MW00454535

A Family Business Publication

Family businesses encounter a unique set of challenges, ranging from strategic growth to succession planning to communication between colleagues (and relatives!). The books in Palgrave and the Family Business Consulting Group's family business series provide guidance on how to overcome them and achieve continued growth and success. The authors are experts in the field, sharing practical, effective, and time-tested insights from their many years running their own family businesses.

Family Wealth Continuity
Building a Foundation for the Future

David Lansky

palgrave
macmillan

David Lansky
Chicago, Illinois, USA

A Family Business Publication
ISBN 978-1-137-57638-5   ISBN 978-1-137-57639-2   (eBook)
DOI 10.1057/978-1-137-57639-2

Library of Congress Control Number: 2016939254

© The Editor(s) (if applicable) and The Author(s) 2016
This work is subject to copyright. All rights are solely and exclusively licensed by the Publisher, whether the whole or part of the material is concerned, specifically the rights of translation, reprinting, reuse of illustrations, recitation, broadcasting, reproduction on microfilms or in any other physical way, and transmission or information storage and retrieval, electronic adaptation, computer software, or by similar or dissimilar methodology now known or hereafter developed.
The use of general descriptive names, registered names, trademarks, service marks, etc. in this publication does not imply, even in the absence of a specific statement, that such names are exempt from the relevant protective laws and regulations and therefore free for general use.
The publisher, the authors and the editors are safe to assume that the advice and information in this book are believed to be true and accurate at the date of publication. Neither the publisher nor the authors or the editors give a warranty, express or implied, with respect to the material contained herein or for any errors or omissions that may have been made.

Cover illustration: © Bercutt/iStock/Thinkstock

Printed on acid-free paper

This Palgrave Macmillan imprint is published by Springer Nature
The registered company is Nature America Inc. New York

Contents

Chapter 1   Introduction   001

Chapter 2   Learning Capacity   017

Chapter 3   Familyness   041

Chapter 4   Safe Communication Culture   065

Chapter 5   Commitment to Personal Development   093

Chapter 6   Effective Leadership of Change   117

Chapter 7   Putting It All Together   143

Index   155

Acknowledgments

This book is the culmination of several years of thinking and writing about the topics in question.

I have had the privilege of discussing the concepts and ideas here over the years with generous and intellectually curious people who have given their time, energy, and genuine consideration to our dialogue. I am deeply indebted to many such thought partners, but I name some of the most influential here: John Duncan, Bryan Dunn, Thayer Willis, Jay Hughes, Dennis Kessler, and Paul Koprowski.

My partners and colleagues of The Family Business Consulting Group have been an amazing source of inspiration, support, creativity, education, and conversation. I am especially grateful to Steve McClure, who provided thoughtful feedback and suggestions on all of the contents.

My wife Jane Jansen has been my closest confidant and coach; I would not be where I am today without her.

Laurie Harting and the team at Palgrave Macmillan were instrumental in shaping, refining, and bringing the book to life. Michael Mok provided masterful work on the graphics.

Many thanks to Sachin Waikar, whose counsel, guidance, and collaboration have been indispensable in developing and articulating the ideas expressed here.

Finally, I have been privileged to work with a great many successful, intelligent, creative, energetic, and vulnerable families who have welcomed me as a consultant and invited me to be a part of incredibly important processes of growth and adjustment in their businesses and lives. Their stories have been an inspiration, and I am forever indebted to them.

CHAPTER 1

Introduction

As an introduction to the topic of the Foundation for Family Wealth Continuity, consider two very different family business situations:

Members of one family attended a national family business conference, where they participated in a day-long workshop to learn about different governance structures and processes. Upon returning from the conference, the family discussed and began to develop several governance measures—including a family council, a plan for management succession, and a plan for passing on family ownership—and started implementing these plans soon after. Taken together, these elements constituted the family's wealth continuity plan and they soon witnessed stronger family relationships together with the overall optimistic view that the business and other family assets would be preserved across generations.

Members of second family worked with several financial/legal advisors and consultants over several months to think about wealth continuity planning. One of the advisors' main recommendations was for the family to create a family council including representation of cousins from all family branches, and to harness the council to aid in succession and ownership transfer planning. While the cousins agreed with the general idea of such a council, they could find no common ground regarding its specific elements—including size, election processes, and others—and it became clear they did not think of themselves as a well-connected "clan," as they struggled to even communicate about simple topics, much less to develop complex plans together. The hoped-for continuity plans never came to be.

These examples, taken from a combination of several business families I've observed, highlight an important reality: while most business families and families of wealth hope to perpetuate their wealth across generations, their ability to do this successfully varies dramatically from family to family. The goal of this book is to help families understand and improve their specific nature on several key dimensions of communication, interpersonal interaction, culture, and leadership related to wealth continuity planning—from their collective capacity to learn, to individual members' commitment to self-development. Together, these "building blocks" make up what I call the Foundation of wealth continuity.

The Challenge of Wealth Continuity Planning

As suggested by the examples above, most family business owners and wealth creators share an important vision: perpetuating the wealth their enterprise has generated for many generations to come. In this context, "wealth" means not only collective financial assets, but also less tangible resources such as family relationships (within and between generations), harmony, and engagement.

To promote wealth continuity, many family wealth creators put into place structures, plans, and processes, including estate plans (which may include diverse trusts), succession plans, governance structures/strategies, and others. Such well-established, systematic components, described in detail later in this chapter, would seem to work to preserve family wealth, at least in theory. In reality, for many families, they don't.

There is growing evidence that wealth continuity planning is not working for many families. Part of the problem is a failure to plan in the first place. A PnC Bank survey of nearly 600 business owners found that while most expected their company and related assets to stay in the family for generations, the majority hadn't developed plans to make this a reality.[1] More directly to my point, a study by Williams and Preisser estimated that among a large sample of affluent clients, 70% of instituted estate plans failed, largely as a result of family conflict or communication problems.[2] This shows that just because families create elaborate plans, success of implementation is not assured.

Overall, there is no consensus, empirically or anecdotally, on why continuity planning fails. I have had countless personal conversations with fellow

---

[1] PNC Wealth Management, "Wealth and Values Survey: Business Owners and Their Path to Happiness," February 2008, https://content.pncmc.com/live/pnc/personal/wealthmanagement/WM_WlthVal_teens_0507.swf (accessed June 5, 2015).
[2] Roy Williams and Vic Preisser, *Preparing Heirs: Five Steps to a Successful Transition of Family Wealth and Values* (Robert Reed Publishers, Bandon, Oregon, 2010).

consultants, attorneys, wealth advisors, insurance professionals, and family business board members centered around one specific question: *How do you know that a particular family will successfully implement a specific wealth-continuity strategy, with lasting results?*

The responses I hear almost always start with "That's a really good question!" followed by some vague factor that may help promote successful continuity planning. Among the more common factors mentioned are:

- "Strong leadership"
- "Altruism"
- "Lack of greed"
- "Lots of money"
- "Trust"
- "Good communication"

But the conversation usually ends with some form of "I don't really know."

Despite the ongoing lack of clarity on the factors promoting effective continuity planning, some in the field have proposed related strategies to communicate more strategically about planning. Recently, for example, some family business and family wealth experts have aimed to enhance continuity planning by encouraging business families, families of wealth, and their advisors to focus on articulating and defining family values and objectives better, *before* focusing on continuity-related tactics.[3] For example, a family might be asked to undertake an exercise to identify their values through a reckoning of past and present actions, and then to use what they discover (such as a focus on stewardship or philanthropy) to inform continuity planning.

While such efforts are important and admirable, they fail to take into account a key factor in the success of continuity planning: each family's unique interpersonal matrix, which serves as the foundation for any wealth-related planning.

---

[3] See for example James Hughes, *Family Wealth—Keeping It in the Family: How Family Members and Their Advisers Preserve Human, Intellectual, and Financial Assets for Generations* (Bloomberg, New York, 2004) and Lee Hausner, *The Legacy Family: The Definitive Guide to Creating a Successful Multigenerational Family* (Palgrave Macmillan, New York, 2009).

One Size Does Not Fit All

Many formal and informal approaches to understanding the success of wealth continuity planning make a faulty assumption: that all families start with a similar pre-existing capacity, or foundation, for developing and implementing a continuity plan. My experience suggests that's a significant problem, because it prevents families and those who advise them from examining the *idiosyncratic* factors that can interfere with continuity planning.

For example, say a family member decides that a specific family governance structure—such as a family council—would be a good thing for her family. Does that necessarily mean that the structure in question is indeed appropriate in that particular family's current context? Similarly, is it fair to assume that an advisor's suggestion to a family, to develop better communication about their values to aid in estate-planning, can be followed easily by that particular family at that particular time?

The answer to both queries is a resounding "No!" The reality is that families differ widely in their baseline capacity to implement and benefit from wealth continuity structures. Just like houses, not every family has the same strength of foundation—some have solid platforms to support taking on challenges like governance and wealth continuity planning, and others have much less stable or effectively non-existent foundations, making them less capable of successful planning.

Consider two more examples of family businesses dealing with continuity planning:

- The parents/founders of a successful family business withheld estate plans from their adult children for decades because they didn't want their children's spouses (the daughters/sons-in-law) to be privy to such "personal" information. When the founders passed away, the children inherited significant shared real estate, but they were poorly prepared to deal with the assets because they had no prior knowledge of the inheritance.
- A wealthy multi-generation business family met with the private banking division of a major bank to discuss continuity planning. The meetings resulted in the recommendation of several "best practices" as groundwork for the planning, including the development of a family council and family vision statement. The discussions failed to take into account

that the two senior family leaders hadn't spoken productively to each other in years, and thus they were unwilling to work on the prescribed items in any depth. Not surprisingly, the family achieved no meaningful continuity planning.

In both cases, the families lacked the proper foundation on which to build effective continuity planning, but for different reasons. While that may seem obvious or even intuitive after the fact, too many business families, families of wealth, and their advisors fail to take foundational factors into account—they don't assess the family's capacity to develop and implement a continuity plan. So it's no surprise that many families either fail to develop a meaningful plan in the first place or create a plan that they're not able to implement effectively. Part of the problem is the ubiquity of prescribed "best practices," as suggested by the example above and described in the box below.

The Myth of Best Practices

Some professional service providers latch onto "best practices" as a selling tool for family businesses and families of wealth interested in vehicles for wealth continuity (such as investments or insurance products). After all, the term sounds catchy and promising—how can the "best" be a bad thing? The problem is that by touting best practices to their potential clients, everyone fails to take into account the *fit* between the practice/product and the family making use of it. Because a given practice must be tailored to a given family situation, there is no such thing as one best practice for all. The family context must be considered very carefully before going forward with any continuity plan element.

So, when it comes to wealth continuity planning, taking a one-size-fits-all approach is never ideal. We can think of such planning using a medical analogy. For thousands of years, it didn't really matter whether sick patients followed their doctors' advice: most medical practitioners were more "quack" than healer, and complying with their recommendations might actually have resulted in greater harm than good in many cases. But that situation changed in the twentieth century with the advent of effective treatments in many areas, from penicillin to polio vaccines. These days, failure to seek medical help or follow medical advice could potentially be lethal. In the same way, business families and families of wealth now have many well-established options to choose from when it comes to wealth continuity planning, including dynasty trusts, multi-participant trusts, leadership succession plans, systems of family governance, and others. But just as a given treatment may not work for a given patient—hence the wide range of medications available for diabetes, depression, and many other conditions—a specific continuity plan component may not be suitable for a specific family. Just as a patient must be assessed carefully for preexisting conditions, allergies, other medications being taken, and other factors before starting on a new treatment, so too must a family's current status be examined to understand what type of "intervention" will work best with regard to continuity planning.

The medical analogy raises another important issue related to continuity planning: compliance. It has been well-established that a large proportion of patients (over 50% in some studies) will fail to follow doctors' advice, even when the risks are large.[4] Similarly, families seeking wealth continuity may fail to implement even the simplest, most seemingly suitable plan. So it's important to assess a family's potential to be compliant before any continuity plan is prescribed, and to address related issues as fully as possible.

So what's the Best Plan?

If you understand and accept the idea that continuity planning is a highly individual activity based on the specific foundation that exists or that can be created within a family, think about these questions:

- Can we differentiate families early on as related to their capacity to follow good advice directed toward family wealth continuity?
- Can we use specific strategies to enhance the capacity of those families who may face gaps or deficits in important areas?
- What actions might be taken when families seem less capable of implementing well-suited planning components, even after efforts have been made to enhance their capacity? (This is the compliance issue mentioned above.)

---

[4] For example, a 2013 study by the National Community Pharmacists Association found that 52% of adults surveyed were significantly non-adherent to their medication regimens; National Community Pharmacists Association, *Medication Adherence in America: A National Report*, 2013, http://www.ncpanet.org/pdf/reportcard/AdherenceReportCard_Abridged.pdf (accessed January 23, 2015).

Thus the central question is:

What customized wealth continuity plan is most appropriate in a given family situation, and how can we ensure it is implemented effectively?

This book is primarily about understanding and building a foundation that will help your family develop and implement the best continuity plan. In this context, I want to emphasize the importance of *implementation*. First, there is a tendency for families to want to rush into the implementation stage of continuity planning—entrepreneurial families are doers by definition, after all—without taking a step back to assess their situation and how that will shape the optimal continuity plan. So I urge all families to proceed carefully and deliberately in this area, getting to know themselves better and formulating a customized strategy that has a higher likelihood of success before acting.

It's largely about understanding the difference between strategy and tactics. As an example, consider a very wealthy business-owner I know—worth literally hundreds of millions of dollars—who feels poor. He feels that way because he set a plan for his wealth to last generations, but then found the plan prevented him from carrying out other important objectives, such as donating a large sum to build a healthcare facility in his hometown. "That won't work with your plan," his financial advisors have told him repeatedly. So in this case, the family business owner mistook a tactic—developing a continuity plan to keep the wealth in the family long term—for a strategy, and then felt constrained by the tactic. The better strategy would have been to have impact on both family and the community, which would have allowed for both a continuity plan and a larger focus on philanthropy. The important thing, then, is to ask not just *what* plan will be best, but also *why* you are creating a plan in the first place.

Second, some people seem to think that good ideas related to continuity planning will automatically implement themselves. That is, if they agree collectively to a few plan elements, then the hard part is done. In reality, while good ideas are a "dime a dozen," and there are many continuity-plan elements out there (and, in some cases, people eager to sell them to you), the harder part of the work is in the implementation, and the family needs specific capabilities to do that successfully. Here again, careful assessment of the family's condition—as related to communication, Learning Capacity and other factors—related to implementation of continuity planning is paramount.

The further challenge is that understanding which factors to assess related to continuity planning and implementation is not easy. In fact, the goal of this book is to help families consider several related factors and to build more effective continuity plans and strategies based on their assessment. So the best approach when it comes to continuity planning is to step back, assess the family carefully on several capacity-related dimensions, and then develop a customized wealth continuity plan that has the greatest chance of creating value for the family in many areas.

Doing that successfully requires an understanding of what I think of as the Foundation for family wealth continuity. Rather than representing an abstract, monolithic platform, the Foundation is made up of several mutually reinforcing "building blocks," as I will discuss in a moment. But first let's consider the specific and shared nature of wealth continuity structures.

Wealth Continuity Structures

In this book I will use the term "wealth continuity structures" to refer to plans, processes or entities designed to preserve family assets while ensuring multi-generational family engagement with the assets.

- *Estate planning structures* including multiple forms of trusts; for example, a dynasty trust is a long-term wealth preservation plan that leaves family assets to future generations and is intended to last "forever".
- *A leadership/ownership succession plan* that stipulates who will lead the business or how shares of the business will be passed between generations.
- *Family governance structures and strategies,* such as a family council, family meetings, and family constitutions.
- *A private family foundation,* that guides philanthropic and other community support efforts while also promoting collaboration between family members outside of business operations.
- *A family office,* or an entity that serves the needs of family members by guiding the deployment of wealth through investments and other vehicles (as a side note, a colleague always says, "If you've seen one family office, you've seen one family office," to highlight the diversity of this entity among family enterprises).
- *A private trust company,* which takes the idea of a family office one step further by acting as a formal trustee for family trusts, making decisions related to investment and allocation.

It's important to understand that these wealth continuity structures share some common elements, including:

1. *Change*: Wealth continuity structures typically introduce some change in how things are currently being done relative to the assets in question. For example, creating a dynasty trust for the benefit of future generations requires that some portion of a family's assets be placed under the control of trustees. Similarly, developing a family council will mean that a family's voice is no longer a function of how "loudly" a given family member or group speaks, but will now be shaped by a more formal collective.

2. *Generational transition*: Continuity structures represent an effort to manage generational transition in control over assets. Whether the structure is a component of estate planning, and therefore stipulates a transfer of assets directly to or beneficially to future generations to reduce estate taxes, or the structure is a succession plan outlining who will lead the business among the rising generation, they are all focused on shifting control, responsibility, or benefit from leading generations to other parties, including trustees or future generations.

3. *Vision of sharing*: They are founded upon a family's vision of sharing assets or control of assets.

4. *Long term*: The continuity structures involve formulating and implementing a long-term plan that prescribes certain desired behaviors and outcomes for generations.

5. *Preservation*: They aim to preserve and grow monetary and non-monetary wealth for the future.

This means families who create wealth continuity structures to perpetuate assets, ensure harmony, and sustain engagement must be able to implement change, accept generational transition in control, articulate a meaningful shared vision, and commit to and carry out a long-term plan. Not an easy set of tasks for almost any family!

Moreover, many families tend to place excessive emphasis on the money and tax liability elements of wealth continuity planning. While that's completely understandable, it fails to take into account a critical asset: the family itself. That is, continuity is as much or more about family relationships and harmony as it is about financial wealth. The families that understand the need to preserve these intangible assets over generations tend to be more successful with planning and its implementation.

A Word on Simplicity

In wealth continuity planning and many other domains there is often a tendency to make things more complex than they need to be. That's almost never the best route to effective solutions and satisfying outcomes. Consider, again, a medical analogy: A variety of studies suggest that greater complexity of a given intervention—how many drugs or dosages or schedules it involves—will interfere with compliance with that treatment.[5]

Therefore, the most effective regimes are typically those that are the simplest. This holds true for continuity planning, as well, where the goal should be to create plans that require the least amount of adjustment by families. Or alternatively, we would want to provide sufficient guidance and support to help families wade through plans that are very complex.

When to Change the Plan, Not the Family

It would be nice to assume that all families can address all issues related to their group dynamics and other challenges. But I recognize fully that some families will struggle with addressing the specific building blocks (elements of the Foundation for Family Wealth Continuity as detailed later in this chapter) in the chapters to follow. Some families just don't have the right "ingredients" to develop strong Learning Capacity for example. Others may never be able to develop what I call a Safe Communication Culture.

In such cases, it is better to change the *continuity plan*, rather than to try to change the family. That may not be the optimal solution, but it is better than having no plan at all, or a seemingly sound plan that will be an ongoing struggle or impossible to implement. As such, in each of the building block chapters that follow I present a section on how to work around that particular component if it seems unlikely the family will be able to improve sufficiently on it. This will involve changing the continuity plan to better reflect the family's situation, dynamics, and potential to change (or lack thereof).

---

[5] For example, non-compliance with complex exercise regimens was found to be as high as 70%; see R.K. Dishman, "Compliance/adherence in Health-related Exercise," *Health Psychology*, 1982, 1, 237–67.

Who Will Benefit from This Book

As a practical guide to enhancing a family's capacity and capability related to wealth continuity, this book is for families and their advisors who wish to perpetuate multi-dimensional family assets, including financial holdings, relationships, and harmony.

Specific groups who will benefit from the ideas here include:

- *Business families and families of wealth* who wish to implement continuity plans and want to enhance their effectiveness and performance on many levels.
- *Estate planning attorneys* who want to evaluate their client families' capability to implement specific wealth transfer structures.
- *Trustees* who seek insight as to strengths and challenges they may encounter as they work with a family to put into practice trust provisions.
- *Advisors* who want to enhance their understanding of family dynamics related to continuity planning and other areas.
- *Financial planners and insurance professionals* who want to align asset management strategies with their family clients' needs and capabilities and help their clients put the strategies into action successfully.
- *Family business board members* who want to help the owning family develop and implement effective continuity plans.

My Background and the Cases in This Book

The ideas and advice I present here are based on 30 years of experience with families and family businesses—the earlier 15 years as a family therapist and the last 15 years as a family business consultant working on issues related to continuity planning, governance, relationships, and many others. In total I have worked with hundreds of families, helping them achieve greater continuity on every dimension.

Moreover, in every instance, the cases I will describe represent *composites* of family business situations I have observed, rather than specific families.

What's in this Book?

As I hope I've made clear by this point, while there's no shortage of sound advice regarding continuity planning, many families fail to develop a plan

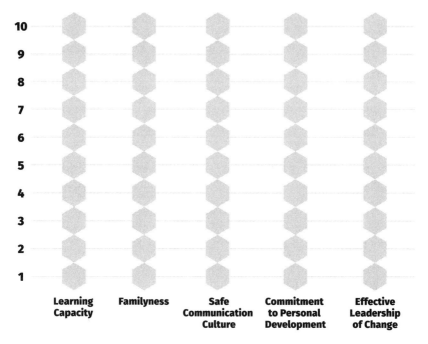

Fig. 1.1 A Foundation For Family Wealth Continuity: The Building Blocks

in the first place or struggle to implement a plan because they lack the prerequisite capacity for doing so. Understanding, assessing, and addressing these prerequisites *prior* to developing and implementing wealth continuity structures is critical. Taking these steps should result in greater likelihood of planning success. Moreover, it's important to remember that this book is about starting a conversation about family wealth continuity planning, rather than delivering "set-in-stone" solutions for you to follow. *My goal is to get you thinking about how to assess and improve the Foundation for Family Wealth Continuity in your family or in one you advise.*

This introductory chapter has served to familiarize readers with the reasons many families struggle with continuity planning—primarily the lack of a foundation on which to build successful efforts. The next chapters will cover in detail what I call the "building blocks" of that foundation: five interrelated features that help families succeed with continuity planning. While these may not be the only relevant factors for continuity, they are the most critical in my experience, as confirmed not only by colleagues but also by the outcomes of the families I have observed or helped.

The building blocks, presented briefly below, will vary in presence and robustness across families, yielding a specific foundational profile for each family, as suggested by Fig. 1.1 (where each block's strength is rated on a scale from 0 to 10). Understanding the nature of their profile will help families address areas of deficit, to provide the strongest continuity planning foundation possible. Each of the following chapters details one building block, including ways of assessing its strength and approaches to improving it.

- *Learning Capacity*: Learning Capacity is about a family system's ability to learn or to adapt to new information and experience, and to communicate newly acquired learning throughout the system. In short, this involves an ability to adapt to changing circumstances with thoughtfulness, insight, and strategy, whether related to wealth continuity planning or other areas of family functioning.
- *Familyness*: Familyness reflects a general sense of goodwill and caring among members such that they enjoy spending time together, trust one another, and are willing and able to give one another the benefit of the doubt. A healthy level of Familyness underlies more stable families and allows them to take risks related to both personal (such as sharing difficult feedback) and business (creating succession plans, for example) dimensions—critical for continuity planning.
- *Safe Communication Culture*: A Safe Communication Culture within a family comprises several elements including comfort with honest dialogue, an ability to accept personal responsibility in difficult issues including conflicts and failures, and a variety of opportunities and forums—both formal and informal—in which members can discuss issues directly and thoroughly. Such a culture provides space and encouragement for the often difficult conversations that take place around continuity planning, boosting mutual understanding and benefit.
- *Commitment to Personal Development*: A family that is committed to personal development emphasizes developing the individual capabilities of members in three key areas: financial/legal literacy, emotional intelligence, and health and happiness. Gaining capacity in these areas ensures members can contribute to wealth continuity in meaningful ways that reflect their own interests and those of the family, integrating these into a coherent vision and plan.

- *Effective Leadership of Change*: Effective Leadership of Change occurs at the individual and collective levels within a family, to promote better alignment among members' interests/skills, the family's vision of its future and that of the business, and the development/ implementation of structures to bring that vision to life. As such, effective leadership addresses many areas of family life from who controls the assets to what communication protocols the family should observe.

Following the chapters related to each building block, I present a final chapter that will help readers understand how to put everything together to create the strongest foundation for wealth continuity possible, by understanding their specific profile, as represented by the pattern of strengths and weaknesses among building blocks.

As a final note, let me point out that while I believe strongly in the value of this book's content, it is not intended as a training manual in family dynamics or wealth planning. I provide guidance and information on how to think about the elements of the Foundation for Family Wealth Continuity but that's not equivalent to complete training in addressing the building blocks and associated family dynamics. An unfortunate outcome would be readers attempting to implement some of the ideas presented here without proper background, guidance, or context. This could lead to experiences of failure with accompanying disappointment, and then giving up on promoting positive change in the family. Rather, the material presented here is intended as a *starting point* for your thinking and conversations, along with grounding for practical steps you may take toward improvement, with outside help and input as necessary.

Points to Remember

Here are the key points from this introductory chapter on the Foundation for Family Wealth Continuity.

- While members of business-owning families and families of wealth frequently understand the importance of wealth continuity structures many fail to develop plans or to implement them effectively.
- This failure may happen because families and their advisors make the faulty assumption that the family has a basic *capacity* to develop and

implement a continuity plan. In reality, families vary widely on the strength of their continuity planning building blocks, and insufficient or absent building blocks will result in failed (or missing) continuity plans.

- Understanding the best plan to implement—and implementing it effectively—requires understanding not only the types of wealth continuity structures available (including estate planning elements and leadership/ownership succession plans) but understanding as well that continuity plans promote change in a family and require shared vision and long-term thinking. Moreover, families need to think about both their strategy (*why* they want to achieve certain goals with their wealth) and the tactics (*what* plan they want to use) to make that strategy a reality.
- Family members and directors, estate planning attorneys, trustees, and others will be able to develop and implement more effective plans by understanding and enhancing the five mutually reinforcing building blocks of a Foundation for Family Wealth Continuity as presented in this book: Learning Capacity, Familyness, Safe Communication Culture, Commitment to Personal Development, and Effective Leadership of Change. At the same time, this book is not intended as a training manual, but rather as a starting point for important ideas and conversations.

CHAPTER 2

Learning Capacity

In this chapter we will discuss the first and most central building block in the Foundation for Family Wealth Continuity Learning Capacity. Without substantial Learning Capacity, your family or a family you advise is likely to struggle to implement wealth continuity structures intended to keep the family together. As an introduction to the concept of Learning Capacity, consider the basic facts about two business families who created wealth continuity structures—in these cases, estate plans—that were intended to benefit their families, but eventually faced frustrating circumstances.

The Scott

Arnold and Mary Scott started a tax software business in the mid-1980s. At the time, they had three children—all under the age of 10—and were advised soon after launching the company to "sell" about 8 % of it to each of the children, for a total of 25 %. At the time, the company was valued at approximately $50,000, so the share each child held was worth very little, about $4000, or not much more than the paper the stock certificates were printed on! Moreover, the low valuation meant very little tax liability associated with the transaction, so the strategy was seen as part of a smart early estate plan.

The children's shares went into a trust managed by Susan, a good friend of the family. The Scotts asked Susan to be the trustee because they trusted her, she had worked as an accountant, and frankly, they didn't know many other people who could fill the role at the time. Susan, for her part, was happy to be the trustee, and she, like the Scotts, thought the role would involve very little active management, given the company's small size.

They were wrong. The market for personal finance software grew tremendously over the next decades, as did the company the Scotts had started. The family business, once valued at only $50,000, grew to tens of millions of dollars in annual revenue, and a ballooning valuation to match. The Scotts were so overwhelmed by their growing business, they never stopped to update those trusts they created years ago. By 2007, when the Scotts decided to sell the company to a large global competitor, it was worth well over $500 million, and the children's trusts, representing 8% of the company each, were valued at about $40 million.

As the company had grown, Susan, the family friend and trustee, had struggled to fulfill her role, often disagreeing with the children—now young adults—about their planned purchases, whether real estate (she was reluctant to approve the purchase of an upscale but very affordable townhome one of the Scott children wanted) or automobiles (she urged them to consider "sensible" cars like Hyundais over luxury brands like BMW and Lexus). As the children grew increasingly frustrated with the situation and Susan became more and more overwhelmed by her responsibilities, the family knew they had to address the problem as soon as possible.

The Rappaports

Ernie Rappaport made a fortune speculating in the real estate markets of major cities including New York and Chicago in the 1970s. As his assets grew, he and his wife created trusts for their two sons. Just as in his business dealings, Ernie took great care with the details of these trusts, appointing several attorneys as trustees and stipulating very tight control over investment and distribution terms. "I want this money to last for generations, so that you and your children and your children's children will all be able to share the benefits and the responsibilities," he told the trustees and his sons. The terms Ernie helped develop for the trusts maximized their growth potential, partly through the restrictions he placed on access.

By the early part of the new millennium, the trusts were worth hundreds of millions of dollars. But rather than being pleased by their good fortune, the Rappaport sons were miserable. Though now in their 40s, they had little say about the wealth that was theirs on paper. For example, while they had been able request distributions from the trusts since reaching adulthood, the strict terms their father had instituted limited severely the frequency and size of any distributions. One of the sons was particularly interested in philanthropy—he volunteered with several non-profits that worked with children with disabilities and terminal illness—but was unable to donate much money to any causes because of the constraints. "It's like we have everything and own nothing," one of the sons said.

When the sons approached the attorney-trustees about loosening the terms, the trustees' response was always the same: "This was not the grantor's wishes." Both younger-generation Rappaports knew that following the attorneys' advice was unlikely to yield what they hoped, and their ongoing dissatisfaction with the situation strained family relations.

I started the chapter with these two stories to create context for the first building block of the Foundation for Family Wealth Continuity Learning Capacity. Without a capacity to learn and transmit new information among members, families will struggle with continuity planning, failing to learn from a variety of sources.

What Is Learning Capacity?

In his popular 1990 book *The Fifth Discipline*, Peter Senge described a "learning organization" as one that promotes organizational learning at many levels.[1] David Garvin expanded on this concept shortly after that book was published, in a *Harvard Business Review* article.[2] According to Garvin, a learning organization is one that is skilled at creating, securing, and transferring knowledge, and at modifying its behavior to reflect new knowledge and insights. He discussed how learning organizations excel at five interrelated activities:

- Systematic problem-solving
- Experimentation with new approaches
- Learning from their own experience and past history

---

[1] Peter M. Senge, *The Fifth Discipline* (Doubleday, New York, 1990).
[2] David A. Garvin, "Building a Learning Organization," *Harvard Business Review*, July 1993.

- Learning from others' experience and best practices
- Transferring knowledge quickly and efficiently throughout the organization

Although the learning organization concept has been applied primarily in business settings, two essential qualities of a learning organization—the capacities *to learn from experience* and *to communicate newly acquired knowledge from multiple sources throughout the organization*—are critical for families who implement wealth continuity structures that are intended to keep the family together or that rely on family collaboration. In other words, families, whose plans successfully keep the family together while sharing assets for generations, demonstrate the capacity to adapt to changing circumstances thoughtfully and strategically. They create opportunities for family members to learn from one another's experiences and to pass on, within and between generations, the lessons acquired. In this way the family demonstrates the Learning Capacity to create and enact its continuity plans.

You will recall from the first chapter that wealth continuity structures intended to keep family together—a business succession plan, an estate plan, a family office or family foundation—introduce change to a family system: change in how assets are managed, change regarding who holds control over different assets, and change in expectations for how family members will work together to promote wealth continuity. A family that manifests a good level of Learning Capacity will respond to this change not with avoidance or rash decision-making driven by individual members' agendas, but with the ability to receive, integrate, and adapt to new information, ideas, and practices, along with communicating what's learned—and its implications for the family—in a strategic way.

In fact, Learning Capacity is so critical to successful family wealth continuity that it may be considered the *cornerstone* of the foundation for successful planning, and thus is the first of the five building blocks we will discuss, as illustrated in Fig. 2.1.

As mentioned above, all continuity plans introduce some form of change, and the ability to accept and adapt to that change—your Learning Capacity is fundamental. Time and again, I have observed that family wealth continuity structures are only as strong as the Learning Capacity or lack thereof—the family has established. Accepting and integrating new information related to wealth continuity structures, along with transferring it to a broad variety of stakeholders—such as shareholders siblings, and in-laws —is paramount. In short, if the goal is to keep family *and* assets together, even the most robust continuity structures will not function as intended without a strong Learning Capacity in place.

The Danger of Suboptimal Learning Capacity

Families with incomplete, absent, or illusory Learning Capacity suffer negative consequences in many important areas. As an example, let's return to the Rappaport family described earlier, in which the sons, now in their 40s, had little access to the family wealth, due to the strict terms their father Ernie had established for their trusts. Their protests about the situation went unheard and, in fact, made their father even more resolute about his stance. The circumstances not only stifled the sons' growth and independence, but also strained family relations, to the point that the younger men were effectively estranged from their father, interacting with him only when it was absolutely necessary or at their mother's request. The extended family also took sides, with a major-

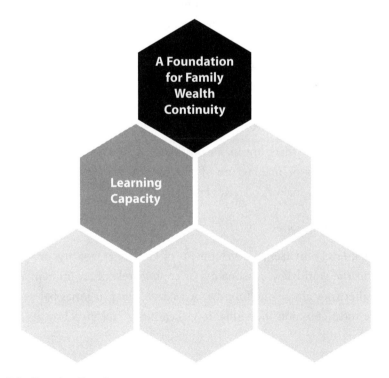

Fig. 2.1 Learning Capacity

ity of members supporting the younger generation's point of view. Thus, an estate plan intended to benefit family members for generations and to engage them in collective wealth management had the effect of pushing people apart and disengaging them from the assets which were to be for their benefit.

There is broad support among family wealth experts for the importance of customizing wealth transfer plans to the unique circumstances of a family and its individual members.[3] This clearly did not happen in the Rappaport family. The absence of options results in a counter-intuitive situation for those with large paper-based wealth: many lead lives of sad desperation, feeling they have no control or sense of value in the world. A family's inability to learn from experience, feedback, and the situations of others is a prime contributor to these unfortunate situations. The Rappaport founder was especially resistant to change and unresponsive to his sons' very vocal feedback and even that of the extended family. His personality and actions made it impossible for the family to adapt to their circumstances, and led to dissatisfaction for the immediate family and perhaps for generations to come. Poor Learning Capacity will almost always result in poor outcomes with regard to wealth continuity structures that are intended to keep families and their assets together.

We can contrast the Rappaport family's outcomes to the much more positive ones of the Scott family. The Scotts improved their circumstances—which looked very much like those of the Rappaports, initially—by using its nascent, strong Learning Capacity to drive meaningful positive change.

Obstacles to Building Learning Capacity

Within any family there are many possible obstacles to building a strong Learning Capacity or making use of that already in place. These obstacles occur at the individual or collective level:

Individual-Level Obstacles

Individual-level obstacles to development of Learning Capacity are typically rooted in the worldview, personality, or coping style of an influential family member (not always the founder or leader). The categories below represent the most common individual-level Learning Capacity obstacles I have observed.

[3] See for example James Hughes, *Family Wealth: Keeping It in the Family* (Bloomberg, New York, 2004).

A rigid worldview

It is certainly not uncommon for wealth creators to develop continuity plans that rigidly reflect their values. After all, it is their wealth to begin with and they have every right to do with it as they please! Moreover, it is not uncommon for a wealth creator to want the family to benefit and to stay engaged: to understand trusts and family agreements, to abide by them, and to participate in meetings of a family office or a foundation. However, engagement, participation, and understanding are dynamic processes that by their very nature require adaptation to the specific qualities of individuals involved. Moreover, rising generations today, including Millennials, expect greater inclusion, participation, and transparency in work-related matters and expect that their voices will be heard about matters that affect them personally. When a family has substantial Learning Capacity, those voices are heard, acknowledged, and integrated in a planning process.

Ernie Rappaport, from our earlier example, held a rigid worldview. This was not all negative: For example, his firm conviction that he had a responsibility to contribute to the welfare of future Rappaport generations led him to establish trusts that grew quickly to a very large size, enabling them to serve future family members well, as he had hoped. At the same time, the elder Rappaport's rigidness represented a problem for the family. Specifically, he believed that while the trusts he established could benefit future generations, the members of each generation should also adhere to his values and professional focus, including those of self-sufficiency (Ernie didn't quite know how to manage the inherent contradiction of embracing self-sufficiency while establishing an intergenerational trust worth many millions) and making money in real estate. Ernie never articulated these ideas fully to his sons, but he clung to his beliefs tightly when he observed their interests did not match his; for example, neither son expressed any interest in real estate as a career focus. Thus Ernie's worldview both led him to create exaggerated constraints on his sons' financial trusts *and* prevented him from seeing the damage caused by these terms, even amidst his children's vocal complaints. He had "taken the trust out of the trust," and his sons increasingly felt trapped, effectively imprisoned by his worldview. When their wives, Ernie's daughters-in-law, took up the cause and tried to intervene, Ernie wrote all of them off as "spoiled," straining family relationships even further.

Not surprisingly, there was very little Learning Capacity in the Rappaport family. Ernie was unwilling to seek, accept, and integrate new information, much less pass this on to other stakeholders. He did not respond in a way that acknowledged the needs of the rising generation and that would properly engage them in a constructive manner around preserving and managing the family's wealth. The younger generation displayed a better capacity to learn, but its members were hamstrung by the patriarch's inflexibility and his control over all major assets. Rather than learning and growing, such families often descend into an abyss of dissatisfaction and animosity, with little interest in deepening relationships and having positive impact within and outside the family. In fact, any growth or positive impact members—especially those of the younger generation—display may occur *despite* the family situation, rather than because of it or as facilitated by it.

Narcissistic individuals

The psychological term "narcissism" is derived from the Greek myth of Narcissus, the son of the river god and a nymph; the boy became a hunter famous for his appealing physical appearance. Rather than being thankful and humble regarding his looks, Narcissus was vain, spurning those who loved him. Nemesis, the Greek goddess of vengeance, observed Narcissus's vanity and lured him to a reflecting pool, where the young man fell in love with his reflection, and drowned.

Narcissism, then, has come to mean damaging vanity, self-love, and self-absorption, as reflected in the simultaneous desire for the admiration of others and the failure to incorporate other's feedback and opinions into one's thinking and self-image, especially if the feedback conflicts with one's beliefs or self-concept.[4] In fact, disagreement with others, however inconsequential, tends to be taken very personally, in the form of what's called a "narcissistic injury." As you can imagine, this type of personality, especially for a family leader, is incompatible with the development of good Learning Capacity,

---

[4] For example, Narcissistic Personality Disorder, as defined by the fifth edition of the *Diagnostic and Statistical Manual* (the "bible" of psychiatric diagnosis), includes both excessive reliance on others for self-esteem and self-definition *and* an inability to have empathy for others or share intimacy with them. American Psychiatric Association, *Diagnostic and Statistical Manual of Mental Disorders (5th ed.)* Arlington, VA. (American Psychiatric Press, 2013).

as that requires significant self-awareness and the ability to integrate others' ideas and emotions into one's own thinking, development, and actions.

Narcissism can be a problem for families whether it's present in leaders or other members. Consider another example of a business family: the owners of a large manufacturing company in the northeastern US, in which all three second-generation siblings worked for the firm. Maria, the middle child, was known for her quantitative analytical skills and quick thinking, which made her a natural successor for an operational leadership role. Unfortunately, she was also known for being difficult, including an inability to tolerate any disagreement or constructive feedback. Maria routinely criticized the ideas of others—including her siblings—and stomped out of countless company and family meetings in a huff when she felt "unheard," "misunderstood," or "ganged up on." Despite the family's repeated efforts to reason with her, she was unwilling to become more accommodating or flexible. Again, the mindset and actions of a single family member prevented adaptation and learning because her behavior stood in the way of constructive feedback that could be used to modify the family and business systems, and the founding generation had to abandon its longstanding plan to have the three second-generation siblings become co-owners who collaborated as business leaders; the parents even discussed selling the business to prevent discord among the siblings. Maria's narcissistic behavior had effectively derailed the continuity plan and led to negative consequences for her in the form of a lost opportunity.

In the study of *thermodynamics*, closed systems are defined as physical systems which do not exchange any matter with their surroundings, and are not subject to forces whose sources are external to the system. The anthropologist Gregory Bateson applied this concept to the study of families and suggested that families can be closed systems in the sense that their growth, evolution, and interactions are isolated from the outside world.[5] When families are closed systems in this sense they have difficulty adapting to change—they have low Learning Capacity because they are insulated from new information.

As the description above suggests, without sufficient capacity among family members for the acceptance of feedback, a family system does not change, and remains closed. Feedback leads to greater self-awareness, flexibility, learn-

---

[5] Gregory Bateson, Don D. Jackson, Jay Haley, and John Weakland, "Toward a Theory of Schizophrenia," *Behavioral Science*, 1956 1(4): 251–254.

ing, and adjustment—all of which drive improvement and growth at the individual and system levels. Narcissism prevents this growth by working against development of Learning Capacity and making individual family members impervious to learning from others. Those with a tendency toward narcissism are fragile and brittle, and their presence in a family system limits severely the potential growth of that system.

Autocratic leadership

Rigid worldviews and narcissistic behaviors can underlie or represent symptoms of autocratic leadership—the concentration of power in the hands of a single leader who gives little or no regard for others' opinions and wishes. "Autocrat," then, is a slightly less blunt word for "dictator." Ernie Rappaport is certainly an example of an autocratic leader, one who exerted inflexible control over the family's continuity plan, to the point that the family imploded.

Another example is Peter Rizzo, the highly successful Italian-American founder of a family-owned retail clothing business. Rizzo placed a large portion of assets into a family foundation, with the goal of supporting two specific causes: (1) The promotion of Italian cultural institutions in the US; (2) Support for university courses on Italian history. While these were valid causes, Rizzo's approach to philanthropy within the family was far from optimal. He made clear that his values were the *only* ones the family should support, and went so far as to write a family charter that specified that (he was the sole author of that document). When his adult children and their spouses, several of whom helped to run and govern the foundation (which Rizzo chaired), said, "What if we want to give to other causes?" Rizzo dismissed their concerns, replying, "It's important to invest in our heritage." All parties became increasingly frustrated, and as it became clear they were at an impasse, the other family members associated with the foundation decided to resign their posts.

In this way an autocratic leader not only fails to learn and adjust based on the inputs of others within and outside the family, but also prevents the development of broader Learning Capacity. As we have discussed, the absence or insufficiency of Learning Capacity makes it impossible in most cases to develop and implement a wealth continuity plan that involves, engages, and truly benefits the family. Notice that in this example, both the extended family and broader society suffered because of the Learning Capacity issue.

Interpersonal Obstacles

In this section we turn to *interpersonal* obstacles to the development of strong Learning Capacity, or those that originate in specific, recurrent interactions or dynamics among family members, rather than stemming from the personality, worldview, or behavior of one specific individual. Here are some of the most common interpersonal obstacles I have observed.

Narcissistic interactions

Narcissism leads to problematic behaviors on the part of *individuals*, but can also result in difficult and damaging dynamics among and between family members, as suggested earlier. Alice Miller's well-known book *The Drama of the Gifted Child* points to a particularly challenging interaction set in motion by a narcissistic parent.[6] Miller argues convincingly that narcissism underlies a process whereby a parent expects his or her child to fulfill the parent's deepest wishes, effectively wanting the child to "mirror" the parent's desires and needs (serving as a reflection of these). This can be an overt or covert expectation.

Children tend to react to this unreasonable explicit or implicit demand in one of three ways, depending on their own personality and situation:

- *Striving to rise to it*: "See how well I'm meeting your expectations by getting an MBA from a top school!"
- *Becoming "numb" and unresponsive*: "I don't care that you want me to get an MBA; I don't really care about anything."
- *Actively seeking* not *to fulfill the parent's wishes*: "You want me to get my MBA so I'm going to quit my job and not even apply to business school!"

Without a particularly high level of self-awareness or social support, children in these situations may demonstrate these unhealthy responses. Moreover, the potential for development of a narcissistic interaction is

---

[6] Alice Miller, *The Drama of the Gifted Child (3rd ed.)* (Basic Books, New York, 1997).

particularly high in the case of the oldest child in the family, as suggested by the "Be My Clone Syndrome" box below.

"Be My Clone" Syndrome

In my experience, in many families, the oldest child—especially if it's a son—is often expected to mirror the wishes and even the personality or style of the founder or wealth creator. The founder and other family members may hope the child will be a "clone" of the leader, reinforcing this idea in subtle and less subtle ways, such as pointing out similarities or frowning on departures related to career interests or leadership style. This effectively becomes a "set-up" with minimal positive consequences: Aside from the fact that "cloning" a wealth creator is quite a challenge, since these people are often exceptional in many ways (even though they may not recognize that themselves), if the child is truly a clone of the parent, then the child can add little value to the family enterprise as his or her views and ideas will be seen as unoriginal and derivative; if the child fails to mirror the parent adequately, he or she becomes a tremendous disappointment to the parent and sometimes the broader family (as related to the concept of narcissistic injury discussed earlier). Many children in this case actively avoid becoming part of the family enterprise, having understood how unrealistic the expectations are. Others may join the enterprise but end up dissatisfied and ultimately depart. Dealing with the pressure of the situation with alcohol or drugs is another common outcome. Moreover, families in which "Be My Clone" syndrome is manifest are more likely to witness problematic sibling or cousin interactions, such as those related to jealousy over the attention paid to the oldest of a rising-generation. The best way to avoid Be My Clone Syndrome is to have better self-awareness on the part of the parent and open communication about the child's interests and capabilities—though this is easier said than done, in most cases.

These interactions will work against a family's Learning Capacity and may undermine wealth continuity structures such as a family office or an estate plan, which are intended to bring the family together in the sharing of assets; in fact, these interactions will actively interfere with the development of the systemic capacity to learn, improve, grow, and collaborate.

Poor intra- or inter-generational communication
Information is passed on through effective communication, and strong communication within and between generations is the vital substrate of learning

capacity. For example, narcissistic and autocratic leadership patterns will result in what I consider "one-way" communication of needs, ideas, and directives, with no real listening or adjustment as part of the interaction. Several factors can impede two-way communication in families:

- *Individual-level obstacles* such as the rigid worldview, narcissism, and autocratic leadership styles discussed earlier lead to communication-related "symptoms" within the family
- *Cultural factors* that lead to strict hierarchy and formal communication—in some families, the cultural origins prescribe so much parental respect and authority that young people feel little freedom to express concerns or disagreement; a slightly different culture-related issue is discussed in the *Sociocultural Diversity* section below
- *Intrafamily factors* including past/current rifts among individuals and/or branches

All of these factors will prevent regular transmission of learning—or much of anything else—across the family system, thus interfering with a family's Learning Capacity.

Sociocultural diversity

While sociocultural diversity in its many respects (gender, geographic, religious) can be of great value to a family, for example, by introducing creative new ideas, or by welcoming family who otherwise might stay out of the fold, some families suffer when members and/or generations have highly diverse sociocultural background experiences, making it difficult for them to understand or communicate with one another. Some family members may literally speak different languages, as cousins may have grown up in different countries than one another or than their parents, and may have adopted not only different languages but new culturally influenced expectations and ways of thinking. This is often the case among first-generation families, who build businesses in their new countries, and among those families whose children are educated overseas and remain there. In some of these cases, the divergence in cultural and social experience prevents the development of genuine communication and understanding, which are required for true learning and adaptation to take place. This may be seen, then, as a special case of the poor communication patterns noted in the previous item.

Promoters of Strong Learning Capacity

As an introduction to the factors that promote Learning Capacity, we return to the Scott family example from earlier in the chapter. You will recall that the family had built and sold a tax software business worth over $500 million, but Susan, the family-appointed trustee, had been at odds with the younger family members over how they wished to use the money in their trusts. It became increasingly clear to both generations that Susan, though well-intentioned, had little capacity to help manage the invested assets in the adult children's trusts, or to educate them about ownership and its implications. The parents were in fact sympathetic to the issue the children faced, in part because the children had communicated their dissatisfaction frequently and respectfully. But shortly after the sale of the business, the family realized they had a complicated problem: because of the way the trusts had been written, it was not possible to remove Susan as the trustee. Early on, the family had given minimal thought to such issues because the business was worth so little at its inception. Now, the terms were a source of ongoing disagreement and frustration.

Unlike the Rappaport family, the Scotts took a much more proactive approach, one fueled by an ability to listen, learn, and act. Through many meetings and conversations the family came to the understanding that because of changing circumstances it no longer made sense to have Susan as the trustee. The Scotts explored options with the help of lawyers and outside consultants, and ultimately took a simple approach: They asked Susan to resign voluntarily, to allow them to hire new trustees who could serve the family's needs more effectively. Susan agreed—she admitted that she had thought about resigning previously, but had felt she would be letting the family down—and things changed quickly as the family enlisted new trustees with the ability to educate the children on the value and implications of the trusts and manage the invested assets more effectively. In this sense, the new, more experienced trustees were able to boost the family's Learning Capacity significantly. As the Scott children gained more knowledge and there was more flexibility related to their trusts, they felt much more satisfied with their lives and the family situation, and this enriched family relationships significantly.

The Scott example highlights how a family's ability to generate and incorporate feedback can help them understand the changing circumstances and needs of members and adapt accordingly. In other words, they rely upon strong Learning Capacity through which to create continuity planning solutions that promote the collective good. Below are several interrelated promoters of strong Learning Capacity.

Embrace feedback

As humans we simultaneously want feedback and try to avoid it. In fact, feedback is related to several of the "10 Reasons People Resist Change" pointed out in a recent *Harvard Business Review* article, including loss of control, excess uncertainty, and concerns about competence.[7] While that's understandable, the families who are most successful at promoting continuity planning and engaging family members tend to manage family dynamics and prepare for future transitions by creating ample space and opportunity for the transmission of feedback. In fact, such families celebrate feedback as a means for enhancing professional and personal performance and relationships, as well as the quality of collaboration—all part of strong Learning Capacity. One of the habits Stephen Covey describes in his seminal *The 7 Habits of Highly Effective People* is "Seek first to understand, then to be understood."[8] Securing and using feedback can be thought of as a habit of highly effective *families*!

Promotion of feedback can be as simple as family leaders asking, "How am I doing?" with regard to their impact on both business and people issues—and then of course listening to the answers. Or the approach can be much more formal, sophisticated, and even institutionalized. I know families that have created comprehensive surveys to tap family concerns on a range of dimensions; they then use the survey results to generate solutions and plans to improve performance. There is no one right method through which to encourage feedback. The most important thing is to be as open as possible to it—not just through "lip service"—and to create real opportunities for the sharing of feedback.

This was part of the challenge for the Scott family. The family had many advisors, and it was recognized that the trustee lacked the capability to serve the family as hoped. But no one was willing to come out and say this, especially at first. Even the children tended to downplay the situation, saying that they were "happy" to have Susan's help but wanted more flexibility. When I work with

---

[7] Rosabeth Moss Kanter, "10 Reasons People Resist Change," *Harvard Business Review*, September 25, 2012, https://hbr.org/2012/09/ten-reasons-people-resist-chang/ (accessed April 27, 2015).

[8] Stephen Covey, *The 7 Habits of Highly Effective People (Anniversary edition)* (Simon & Schuster, New York, 2013).

families like the Scotts, I urge them to provide one another very honest feedback, especially about issues that can be resolved with practical solutions—such as those related to financial trusts. Once the family understood the importance of honest feedback, they were able to move quickly to resolve the situation. The Rappaport family, in contrast, had little capacity for feedback (and thus for learning), due to Ernie's rigid, autocratic style. In fact, any attempt at providing feedback—such as by the sons and their wives—was seen as evidence of disrespect and even "spoiled" behavior. See the "Danger of Yes-But" box for additional thinking on promoters and obstacles related to feedback.

The Danger of "Yes-But"

Many families have what I call a "yes-but" culture, in which members appear to listen to one another but in actuality have little regard for what others think or feel. This is especially the case when it comes to receiving feedback on plans or structures. For example, a family member might say, "I think we need to allow the cousins to have a say in how our assets are managed," and the person listening may respond with "Yes, but they don't have the expertise required." The "yes" is negated immediately by the "but," effectively adding up to a "No." So rather than the conversation leading to a productive dialogue about how best to engage and educate the rising generation, it goes nowhere. A more productive dialogue would be "Yes, and perhaps they can work with us to decide on a good process for their education." The "yes-but" may be symptomatic of a family with poor Learning Capacity, as it signifies minimal appreciation for feedback and, typically, a dearth of self-awareness among influential members. Such families need to work hard at developing more of a "yes-and" culture, in which members not only accept and understand others' suggestions and feelings but build on these with ideas and input of their own. That helps create much stronger Learning Capacity.

Emphasize team learning

Team learning is a critical concept for families who want to establish good Learning Capacity.[9] The idea is that the best approach to family matters that are intended to engage family members is a collective one in which members

[9] Team learning is a well-established organizational concept. For more on the characteristics and benefits of team learning, see Amy Edmonson, James Dillon, and Kathryn Roloff, "Three Perspectives on Team Learning: Outcome Improvement, Task Mastery, and Group Process," *Harvard Business School Working Knowledge*, December 11, 2006, http://hbswk. hbs.edu/item/5566.html (accessed April 27, 2015).

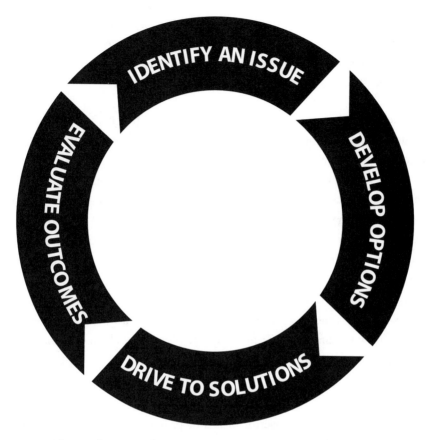

Fig. 2.2 The team learning cycle

work together, using their strengths, experience, and insights. As mentioned earlier, any wealth creator of course has the right to create a wealth continuity plan or structure such as a succession plan or a family foundation that reflects his or her own values and vision; but plans that touch family members or that are intended to be managed by family members are most likely to be implemented properly when families work *together* to educate themselves and to achieve their collective goals. The process drives many benefits including not only the potential for better solutions—because the whole is greater than the sum of its parts—but also the goodwill, the buy-in, and the new shared learning that the family will experience. You can think of it as a simple cycle with the components below, as illustrated in Fig. 2.2.

- *Identify a family issue or objective* (such as developing a Family Council)
- *Work together to develop and pursue options* (such as considering different structures and types of participation for the Family Council)

- *Drive toward strong solutions* (such as creating a Family Council that brings diverse members together for group decision-making)
- *Evaluate what has been learned* from the process and apply that to next issue

Like feedback, team learning can be promoted through a variety of mechanisms, again ranging from casual to highly formal and institutionalized. Family governance structures are particularly valuable in supporting team learning. For example, the presence of a formal family council in a family enterprise creates an excellent opportunity for team learning, as part of the council's agenda will be wrestling with complex issues around estate planning and other topics.[10] Even among families that institute such governance structures, some families will have a more natural ability to engage in team learning than others. Creating a cyclical process such as that described above can be an effective way to facilitate team learning and reap its benefits. For example, the Scotts applied what they had learned from dealing with the trustee issue—such as how to communicate more openly—to future challenges including developing a formal family foundation.

Tell stories

Storytelling has been a powerful means of promoting learning throughout history, from the passing down of ancestral stories orally to the increasing use of narrative in modern-day educational curricula. Story is increasingly used in business settings to establish leaders' credibility, pitch products (such as the way Steve Jobs introduced the iPhone and other Apple products), and seek investment.[11] In the same way, storytelling creates compelling opportunities for the passing of knowledge between generations of a business family or family of wealth. Stories convey the nature and meaning of the founder's values, for example. Narrative can also help later-generation members understand how the family's wealth came about, and how rising generations have used innovation and other practices to maintain and enhance performance.

---

[10] For more on the creation and running of a family council, see Christopher Eckrich and Stephen McClure, *The Family Council Handbook* (Palgrave Macmillan, New York, 2012).
[11] For more on storytelling in business see Roger Dean Duncan, "Tap the Power of Storytelling," *Forbes*, January 4, 2014, http://www.forbes.com/sites/rodgerdeanduncan/2014/01/04/tap-the-power-of-storytelling/ (accessed April 27, 2015).

Transmission of learning through stories is particularly valuable because knowledge passed in this way is much more likely to be remembered than through other means.[12]

Use outside resources
Since, as previously noted, families can become closed systems, and closed systems lack or even avoid outside input, it is important to call on outside resources to enable strong Learning Capacity that supports informed, adaptive continuity planning. Along with infusing new ideas into the system, outside resources can help families embrace change and sometimes even serve as the "bad guy" for particularly challenging issues, such as enforcing greater financial discipline among family members. Some of the most common outside resources in this regard include:

- *Courses and workshops.* There are many providers of educational courses and workshops that address wealth continuity planning, whether a one-day seminar on estate planning or a week-long session on family enterprise governance and leadership. University-based business schools, such as the one at Northwestern University's Kellogg School of Management or the University of Chicago's Booth Graduate School—offer such programs.
- *Books.* Books can be a useful, low-cost way to learn and apply new ideas, including those related to continuity planning.[13] There are many business-focused books, and a growing number that handle family wealth topics specifically.
- *Other families.* One of the best ways for families to learn is from other families, especially those that have dealt with similar issues in the past. The best resources in this instance are families or family businesses who are successfully managing their planning and are willing to share their experiences. Access to these families may of course be limited due to pri-

---

[12] As cited in multiple sources including Sean Blanda, "Want Your Message to Stick? Tell a Story," *99U.com*, http://99u.com/articles/7229/want-your-message-to-stick-tell-a-story (accessed April 27, 2015).

[13] See for example John L. Ward, *Perpetuating the Family Business: 50 Lessons from Long Lasting, Successful Families in Businesses* (Palgrave Macmillan, New York, 2004) and Craig E. Aronoff, Stephen L. McClure, and John L. Ward, *Family Business Succession: The Final Test of Greatness* (Palgrave Macmillan, New York, 2010).

vacy concerns. However, banks and other wealth management organizations occasionally conduct private events that enable sharing at this deep level. Some family business conferences (such as Transitions East and West, hosted by *Family Business Magazine*) provide for a safe, exclusive environment in which families are able to share planning experiences, and personal networks may be another way to reach families who might be helpful.

- *External advisors.* External advisors, whether family business consultants, lawyers, or accountants, can draw on their experience and insights to help with many elements within a wealth continuity framework. While lawyers and accountants can advise specifically on structural aspects of continuity planning (estate plans, how to establish a family office, and the like), family business or family wealth advisors can help promote the development of strong Learning Capacity by providing feedback, encouraging listening and assisting in the adaptation of structures and processes. Not surprisingly, family members are often unaware of their individual and collective strengths and weaknesses—as the saying goes, a fish in the water doesn't know it's in the water until it's *out* of the water. Consultants can take the proverbial fish out of the water to show them patterns they may not be able to observe themselves!

It's About Promoting Change—and Listening

Regardless of how you approach the idea that Learning Capacity is essential to the creation of structures that will engage family members and be properly implemented, the process will require one central element: change. As suggested in the first chapter, accepting and embracing change is a core element in the implementation of continuity plans, and it involves several fundamental components. First is understanding that people may want to change but tend to be resistant to it, whether because of inertia, lack of awareness of alternatives, or some other personal agenda. So expect some resistance, and plan ahead to address it (the subsequent chapter on Effective Leadership of Change addresses this topic specifically). Second, because change requires the acceptance and processing of new information, developing strong Learning Capacity means finding the best ways to integrate new information into your system. How does that happen? By introducing new information—using any of the ideas in this chapter—and getting people to listen. That means offering information in a context that is valued, whether because it is serving the family's collective vision for itself or promoting individual agendas related to financial stability, philanthropy, or other areas.

In fact, one of the simplest but most overlooked actions that families can take to build and benefit from strong Learning Capacity is to practice *listening*. Asking good questions of family members and listening carefully to the answers, rather than simply waiting for a chance to say what's on one's mind, will promote mutual understanding around continuity planning and other elements of a family's wealth or business. Listening, then, can be seen as the foundation for Learning Capacity. As mentioned earlier, seek first to understand, then to be understood. This doesn't mean that people can't disagree; in fact, healthy debate is a hallmark of the families most successful at implementing structures that are engaging and fulfilling, but that can't happen if members fail to listen to one another in the first place.

One of the best outcomes of careful listening will be an understanding of where individual family members stand with regard to their capacity and intent to develop and implement continuity plan elements.

Finally, it should be noted that family members and the consultants who serve them often make the mistake of assuming that all family members have the same capacity to understand and implement complex continuity plans. But this is just not true. Cognitive abilities are multi-dimensional in nature: Some people who are absolute whizzes when it comes to business cannot read past the sixth-grade level. Others may have achieved financial success but struggle with extremely short attention spans. Still others may be musicians or artists who have little or no comfort dealing with financial and legal issues on their own. In that case, they, like patients dealing with complex medical regimens (as discussed in Chap. 1), may misunderstand advice they have been given, not comprehend it in the first place, or forget it altogether. Careful assessment through objective listening—or formal educational assessment methods—can help uncover and address such issues.

Does Your Family Have Strong Learning Capacity?

Answering the following questions will help you understand the strength—or weakness—of your family's Learning Capacity.

- Is there a rush or a sense of urgency when it comes to developing wealth continuity structures that are intended to serve the family broadly?

- Do influential members of your family demonstrate rigid worldviews or narcissistic behaviors that interfere with the ability to provide and receive feedback about plans or intentions?
- Is power concentrated in the hands of a leader or leaders who are unwilling to integrate others' views into important issues and decisions?
- Are there unhealthy interpersonal behavior patterns in your family, such as rigid and unrealistic expectations for later generations to mirror the interests and personalities of preceding generations?
- Are there poor intra/inter-generational communications patterns related to individual personalities, past/current conflict among members, or other factors?
- Are family members, especially leaders, unwilling or unable to hear feedback about their impact on the business or on other people or to listen to others in general (evidence of a "yes-but" culture, for example)?
- Do individual or interpersonal factors prevent team learning, whereby the family identifies issues, works on solutions, and applies what has been learned from the process to the next issue?

Any "yes" answers to the questions above point out obstacles to developing optimal Learning Capacity. The presence of many "yes" answers may indicate a significant problem related to the development of Learning Capacity, and warrants a much closer look at what your family can do to build this critical element of a Foundation for Family Wealth Continuity, using the ideas in this chapter and others in this book.

Where Do You Stand?

In Fig. 2.3, place an X at the point along the column representing "Learning Capacity" to indicate where you think your family stands with regard to the strength of your Learning Capacity. A score of "0" represents non-existent, 10 represent as robust a capacity as possible. You will rate your family's standing on other building blocks in subsequent chapters, to get a sense of how strong your overall Foundation for Family Wealth Continuity is.

When Strong Learning Capacity Is Simply Not Possible

The reality is that not all families will be able to develop strong Learning Capacity (as might be suggested by a very low rating in the section above). This may be due to any of the factors discussed earlier, whether challenging personalities or socio-cultural circumstances. Some families just won't be able to transfer information among members effectively, communicate and accept feedback, and learn from their experience and that of others.

In such cases, it's best for a family to be honest about what is actually feasible, and to develop plans that reflect that reality. For example, if a family's plan includes a family foundation and family members refuse to participate because the foundation's principles have not evolved to reflect more than the founder's values *and* if efforts toward adaptation and integration of others' views have not been successful, inclusion of other family members in this structure may simply not be reasonable. It's one thing for a founder to have a dream of family inclusion, but when the absence of Learning Capacity precludes family participation, the dream may need to be changed or relinquished. This is noted without judgment or criticism: Learning Capacity is fundamental to the dream of family involvement in continuity planning and continuity structures. Sometimes reality transcends dreams.

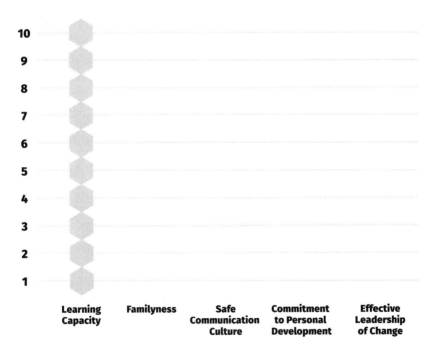

Fig. 2.3 Learning Capacity: Your Rating

Points to Remember

Here are the key points from this chapter on Learning Capacity.

- Strong Learning Capacity helps families communicate within and between generations, accept and apply feedback, and implement continuity structures effectively while adapting to the changes these introduce. Thus Learning Capacity is considered to be essential when wealth continuity plans are directed toward engaging or including family members in wealth transition.
- Major obstacles to building strong Learning Capacity include:
  - *Individual-level obstacles* such as a rigid worldview or narcissistic personality traits among family leaders—these and other factors can contribute to an autocratic leadership style that interferes with Learning Capacity development.
  - *Interpersonal obstacles* including narcissistic interactions (such as the expectation that children will mirror their parents on various dimensions), poor intra/inter-generational communication, and sociocultural diversity.
- Even the simple act of listening can be one of the most powerful promoters of solid Learning Capacity.
- If it's unlikely a family can develop sufficient learning capacity, it may be critical to face that reality and understand that wealth continuity planning might need to de-emphasize family participation. This may be a bitter truth to some, but its recognition and acceptance may help avoid needless frustration and expenditure on dreams unrealized.

CHAPTER 3

Familyness

"Do you love me?"

That's a question that may be asked by family members in some form or other, whether silently or out loud, in any context. But I've heard it come up repeatedly—directly or indirectly, spoken aloud or quietly—in the context of family wealth continuity planning. For example, in a large second-generation family-owned manufacturing business, three siblings who worked in the business became co-owners after their parents passed away. While enthusiastic about owning the business the two sisters and their brother had little interest in collaborating or spending any time together. In fact, that had been the nature of their relationship before their parents passed away; from childhood they had different personalities and interests, and as adults they tended to spend time together only for the sake of their parents. In business, they operated their areas as silos, independent of one another. When together, each complained about the others, whether related to business ideas, work ethic, or perceptions of unfairness regarding ownership (each held an equal share of the business, with various perspectives on the fairness of that arrangement).

"Do you think they love me?" The brother, who acted as CEO, asked me one day in regard to his sisters. "At some level they probably do," I said, "but none of you act it." I pointed out that being a family that gets along most of the time is hard enough, and that adding business ownership/operation to that challenge can be taxing for even the most seemingly well-adjusted group. The broader family—the siblings, their spouses, and their adult children—tried halfheartedly to facilitate more goodwill among themselves, but ultimately realized it wasn't going to happen. The siblings eventually relinquished their operating responsibilities to outside executives, while retaining ownership and board seats. The solution, while not ideal, seemed the only way to maintain the business comfortably within the family.

Family members' interest in spending time together and actually enjoying their togetherness is often a critical factor for family success and wealth continuity. I call this notion Familyness, the next building block in the Foundation for Family Wealth Continuity. When there is insufficient Familyness (as was the case in the example above) or excessive levels of it (as we shall see), a family will face many obstacles to wealth continuity.

What Is Familyness?

The idea of designing family wealth continuity structures that perpetuate assets *and* family harmony is a relatively new economic and behavioral concept. As my colleague John Duncan says, that notion, and the tools and structures that support it, are still in "beta testing."[1] Think about it: Primogeniture, or the practice of passing along all family assets to the oldest son, is perhaps the oldest form of wealth continuity planning, and in many ways the least complex. While primogeniture effectively ensures that the assets will stay together, it more or less guarantees that the family that implements it will not. Promoting family sustainability has never been a primary goal of primogeniture; it seeks, instead, to perpetuate assets in their entirety. That has resulted in countless instances of discord and, historically, even deaths of siblings or, at the very least, their being forced into trades outside the family business.

More modern planning of wealth continuity, then, aims to sustain both assets and less tangible family factors including harmony and goodwill. And that requires Familyness, or a sense of caring and commitment within the family that extends beyond business or other structural requirements. *Familyness* is the next building block in the Foundation for Family Wealth Continuity, as illustrated in Fig. 3.1.

To understand the concept of Familyness fully, we have to place it in the context of family development over time. Specifically, successful wealth continuity plans are often intended to last generations, and thus need to cover families that have expanded dramatically in size, scope, and geography.

[1] John Duncan, personal communication, 2014.

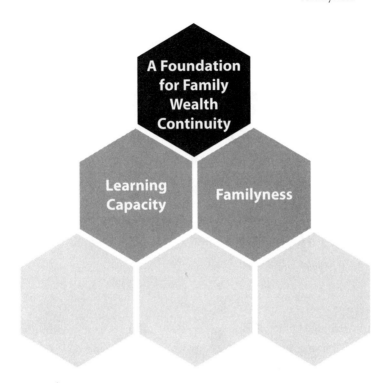

Fig. 3.1 Familyness

As Fig. 3.2 (genogram) illustrates, development begins with a nuclear family (or what we call "G1") consisting of parents and their children. G2, the second generation, represents an extended family that includes spouses, while G3 comprises the children of G2 (first cousins). As the cousins marry and have their own families, the collective family grows to include several or more extended families. Anthropologists refer to the union of several extended families as a "band."[2] By G5, several bands are joined together into a "tribe."

The point is that creating successful wealth continuity structures across this wide a span of time and this large a group of people requires significant *stability* within the family—whether an extended family or a tribe. Just looking at the number of family members in the figure points out the magnitude of the challenge. Moreover, that stability must be based on several supporting personal

---

[2] For more on the evolution of family and other social structures, see Jared Diamond, *The World Until Yesterday* (Penguin, New York, 2013).

Genogram

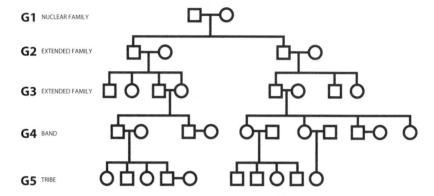

Fig. 3.2 Sample genogram of family development across five generations

and interpersonal characteristics: low levels of "drama", along with high levels of presence, commitment, engagement, and individual and collective satisfaction. Those are all elements of Familyness, perhaps reflected best in the family that says, "We like being together"—and means it.[3] Think of Familyness as having a general sense of caring and goodwill that contains elements of intimacy but lacks the intensity of the intimacy associated with relationships like romantic partnerships. Familyness is also related closely to trust, as individual members feel comfortable relying on one another, sharing personal information, and taking collective risks.

That's not to say that everyone in the family has to enjoy being with everyone else at all times. That's neither healthy nor realistic, as we will discuss later. Harmony may not exist across all generations and within all interpersonal family relationships. But the effort and stability required for successful continuity planning that engages and includes family members is contingent on having *sufficient*—or what could be thought of as "good enough"—care and affection among family members. This typically begins at the "top" of the

---

[3] I am not the first person to present the term Familyness Academics and consultants have used the word to denote the strength of family relationships, among other familial attributes. But a discussion of the most appropriate usage is beyond this book's scope, so I have defined it specifically for our purposes here. Note that I use the term in part because its meaning is intuitive even to those who have never heard it before!

family and permeates the broader pyramidal structure; to promote continuity, Familyness should be present at a collective level (such as the general feel of family reunions), but also evident within a majority of person-to-person relationships within the group.

Why Familyness Matters: A Case Example

A group of cousins—all in their 50s and 60s and living in different parts of the U.S.—were shareholders in a business started by their grandfather. They had been advised by their attorneys to develop a shareholders' agreement, something that had never been part of their ownership arrangement. When first advised to do this, they all agreed that ownership should be held only by direct descendants of their grandfather. However, one cousin learned that in his state there would be considerable advantage to allowing in-laws to own shares, and this made him change his mind about the shareholder agreement.

This was very upsetting to several of his other cousins, and they and their lawyers struggled for many months to arrive at a resolution. Every effort that the attorneys made to find a legal and structural compromise—by revising the shareholders' agreement and estate plans, and by educating family about the possibility of compromise—met with failure.

These cousins were geographically separated from each other and had had little contact with each other over the years. They viewed their shared ownership as a link that held family together and the one cousin's change of mind to allow in-laws to share ownership was viewed as a sort of betrayal of the family. So in reality, no *structural* change in a shareholders agreement or in an estate plan could resolve the situation. That's because the problem was not in the cousins' structures but in their definition of family. In order to arrive at a structural resolution, they would need to revitalize their sense of Familyness: restore trust and intimacy and repair the sense of betrayal that they experienced. So how important is Familyness? In this case, not even the experienced legal minds that were brought to bear on the situation could have an impact until *family* was redefined and Familyness was restored.

Familyness and Self-Development

In Rudyard Kipling's *The Second Jungle Book*, he writes as part of the "Law of the Jungle": "For the strength of the pack is the wolf, and the strength of the wolf is the pack."[4] In other words, the family is only as strong as its members, and the individual members are only as strong as the collective family. For families that share assets, that means living with the paradox of tending to the health of the tribe while also respecting each member's individuality.

That can be a challenge, as not all families will see the tribe as a source of strength. "We are not a tribe," one family business shareholder told me flatly, in describing how family members had grown independently as individuals. In that family, personal-development was seen as a much greater priority than collective growth. Another family shared with me how much they had struggled to maintain relationships across the extended families and individuals within the broader group, sometimes sacrificing individual goals for the collective good, for example when they decided that *no* family member should lead their operating company, as this would introduce further complexity that might undermine the family's Familyness. A non-family CEO was selected instead. That tribe valued the collective over the individual.

Consistent with an ongoing theme of this book, neither extreme on the individual-collective spectrum is ideal. The key is striking a good balance between individual and collective goals and development. While a strong sense of Familyness is essential for families to work together, and to implement wealth continuity structures that are engaging and inclusive, healthy individual development is necessary for family members to contribute meaningfully and with full self-awareness as to the commitments they are making.

As we will discuss later in the book, it's important to understand the difference between personal or self-development and *selfish* development. *Self-development* refers to maturation, self-sufficiency and self-awareness; *selfish development* refers to efforts that are focused exclusively on one's own interests. Only the former contributes to Familyness.

While, as noted, Familyness is essential in providing support for personal-development efforts, too much Familyness will stifle personal development by ignoring or even suppressing individual beliefs and needs, motivating members to seek greater distance from the family, for fear that they will be subsumed or even *consumed* by it.

[4] Rudyard Kipling, *The Second Jungle Book*, available at http://www.gutenberg.org/files/1937/1937-h/1937-h.htm (accessed August 26, 2015).

Too Much Familyness

Ironically, situations involving excessive familyness can sometimes arise from a *paucity* of familyness in a prior generation. Take, for example, the Martinez family, which owns significant real estate holdings in the southwestern US. Juan and Christina Martinez founded the business in the 1970s and were very excited to have their three children join the family firm two decades later.

Spending time together was, in fact, the Martinez' biggest priority. This was the indirect result of Christina's own upbringing within a single-parent family. Christina's mother struggled with alcoholism and depression, which distanced her from her three children. Christina and her two siblings were close in their early years but grew apart as teenagers and had little interaction thereafter, in part because each dealt with their difficult childhood in different ways—Christina's main coping mechanism had been her close friendships, and she envied her friends who came from families that happily spent time together.

Happy families do *everything* together, Christina came to believe. She feared that spending time apart represented a slippery slope, with family members becoming more distant and uninterested in one another, as had happened in her family of origin. Juan, more easygoing by nature, allowed Christina's beliefs to guide most major family decisions. As such, the matriarch's over-compensation for her own experience led to a suffocating level of Familyness for the Martinez family. For example, the children had lived their whole lives in their hometown, including attending a local college—this was a spoken assumption from an early age. Given the success of the family business, the Martinez family had been able to build a large compound including several detached homes, and the second-generation siblings, their spouses, and their young children inhabited these, with the extended family expected to meet for dinner weekly. The family also took almost all vacations together, renting large ski houses and beach houses to accommodate the growing brood. Similarly, any significant decision—personal or professional—was subject to family discussion, with final authority granted implicitly to the founders, who were often critical of choices that they disagreed with or that they believed would reduce family closeness.

Moreover, because closeness was valued over all other qualities, there was little room for candor (including candor about dissatisfaction with the expectation of closeness) that might threaten family cohesiveness or the development of individual interests that might take a family member away from the family for any period of time (such as residing elsewhere or even taking independent vacations, with the exception of a long weekend here or there). All of this closeness was accompanied by a postponement of estate and business succession planning, in part because the planning would likely involve difficult decisions (who will lead the business going forward?) and in part because nobody in the family would take a risk to raise the subject, fearing disruption of the family's harmony.

Factors that drive excessive Familyness can relate to the early experience of an individual in a prior generation—as was the case with Christina Martinez in the example here—or to a combination of personalities present in the nuclear family (such as traits that lead to a pattern of excessive dependency or enabling, as might be the case in a family with a history of alcoholism or addiction among members).

Excessive Familyness may result in what I call "imposed mutuality," a family dynamic in which family members feel compelled to be together by a decision or decisions that have been made by other parties and that may not reflect the choice of all individuals involved. Note that imposed mutuality may have a number of negative consequences including:

- *Resentment* on the part of younger family members because they feel no control over their choices in key domains
- *Underdevelopment of individual interests*, as these may not serve the collective interest
- *Unspoken tensions* related to the items above and other dissatisfaction at the individual and interpersonal levels
- *Explosive disagreements* that surface as a result of the items above, followed by no discussion or gaining of insights related to what caused the disagreement in the first place
- *Discord with in-laws and other "outsiders"* who don't understand the focal family's choices and want more individuality on the part of members—such as daughters/sons-in-law who want to spend the occasional vacation with their own families
- *The presence of medical/psychological symptoms or conditions* including those related to mood disorders (such as depression), anxiety, and substance abuse

Of course, all of these consequences will interfere significantly with inclusive continuity planning, as the planning will fail to represent what family members truly want, and there will be no space for healthy discussion of an appropriate continuity plan. There are also links among Familyness, personal development, and continuity structures, as previewed earlier. Excessive Familyness impedes personal development by stifling individual needs and decisions, especially when these run counter to collective interests. Without personal development and good engagement, continuity—and the structures that facilitate it—loses its purpose, as family members may fail to see any personal meaning in the process. *Why are we keeping our money tied up in trusts for generations?* they might ask, if they see no relevance to meaningful individual pursuits, but relevance only to family members in generations to come. More practically, diminished personal development means that individual members may be less able to contribute to the design and proper implementation of complex continuity plans in meaningful ways.

Too Little Familyness

On the other end of the spectrum is *too little Familyness*, or a lack of significant interest or care for the family as a whole. This was the case in the example discussed in the introduction, where the second-generation siblings had little interest in working together or sharing their lives outside work. A dearth of Familyness can occur for multiple, potentially interrelated reasons:

- *Difficult personalities* among family members, especially those in leadership roles, will attenuate Familyness. For example, this can relate to the rigid worldview or narcissism discussed in the *Learning Capacity* chapter. The presence of such traits or characteristics may make it difficult for family members to get along—as related to unrealistic expectations, for example—and ultimately create distance among members.
- *A history of conflict* between members or family branches may diminish Familyness, even if the original discord took place in earlier generations. For example, a rift between second-generation siblings can be passed down intentionally or unintentionally to their children, who may display little interest in forming an amicable bond with their cousins, the offspring of people who "did their parents wrong." In some cases, past

conflicts can lead to "destructive entitlement," as discussed in the box below.

Destructive Entitlement in Families

The Packers had a problem: Now in its third generation of business ownership (a highly successful manufacturing company), the family struggled with forming and running a family council. Specifically, CEO and board chairman Paul and his cousin Rose (not employed by the business) butted heads repeatedly as council members, preventing anything from getting done. Facilitation by a third party helped Paul and Rose recognize that they were carrying unresolved issues related to their parents' conflict: Rose's father Ted, who had married into the family, had faced significant conflict with Thomas, Paul's father and previous CEO, who had ultimately fired Ted. Rose now understood that she was retaliating against Paul on her father's behalf, and was able to promote a more peaceful relationship—and better family council functioning—after gaining this insight. The Packers' situation is all too common, and a good example of "destructive entitlement," or when family members who feel victimized by past wrongdoings feel entitled or justified to vilify or victimize others. That sense of entitlement may result in a destructive dynamic that can destabilize the family and potentially lead to long-term ill will or estrangement. The new victims—and their nuclear families—may then feel entitled to victimize still others within the extended family, allowing the pattern to repeat within and across generations. Reconciliation, driven largely by acknowledgement of wrongdoing, apologies, forgiveness, and a willingness to proceed, is the best remedy for such situations, resulting in greater alignment in perspectives on past emotional events, healthier relationships, and more effective continuity plans.

The following two factors illustrate the fact that a dilution of Familyness need not be seen as the result of dysfunction but instead as the result of naturally occurring forces that every family must face at one time or another (what Jay Hughes has referred to as "entropy" in a family[5]).

- *Geographic dispersion*, increasingly common in modern, globalized society, makes it difficult for family members, especially those in later gen-

---

[5] James Hughes, *Family: The Compact Among Generations* (Bloomberg, New York, 2007).

erations, to form bonds with relatives, even if they desire this.[6] Although options for connectivity via email, videoconferencing, text messaging, and so on have proliferated, individual family members and their assets may be separated by greater physical distance than ever before. It is difficult, under these circumstances, to nurture and sustain a strong sense of Familyness. Bridging that distance requires interest, energy, and action, and the lack of any of those will necessarily reduce Familyness.

• *Intrafamily diversity*, whether related to gender role, culture, political views, sexual orientation, or other dimensions, is at once a benefit and cost. While families, especially more inclusive, thoughtful ones, can gain knowledge and insights from members' diversity, bridging interpersonal gaps along key dimensions can be difficult, and failure to do so will increase dissatisfaction and decrease Familyness. I had one father tell me flat out he didn't trust his daughter-in-law, who was of another religion, and he refused to allow her any information about the family wealth. In another US-based family a young family member married a Japanese woman. The patriarch insisted on setting up a US-based foundation because in his words, if he didn't, his money would be "headed east." On the positive side, a family based in Central America decided to hold a family meeting in the UK, because that is where their son and new daughter-in-law had settled down. In all of these cases, the challenge was not from a dysfunctional family situation but, as noted previously, from natural forces that result in dispersion and diversity.

Whatever its source, diminished Familyness has many potential negative consequences. I alluded to one of them earlier: stunted self-development. Too little Familyness will fail to provide a solid platform for individual development, including the necessary emotional and practical support members need to pursue their interests and aspirations. That may also result in the failure of individual members to develop the mindset and tools for sophisticated continuity planning. Moreover, a lack of Familyness fails to focus individual members on the collective good and its relation to continuity planning. In other words, if everyone is on their own, why bother developing a strategic

---

[6] Many authors describe the challenge geographic dispersion poses to family structures, including Ross D. Parke, *Future Families: Diverse Forms, Rich Possibilities* (Wiley, New York, 2013).

continuity plan in the first place? Finally, too little Familyness, as noted earlier, may result in tense, brittle family relationships that do not provide a good context for collaboration or honest, open dialogue about important family plans.

Psychiatrist Murray Bowen has discussed self-development in the context of family based on the concept of "differentiation," as discussed in the "Self-Differentiation, Family, and Wealth Continuity" box below

Self-Differentiation, Family, and Wealth Continuity

According to Murray Bowen, how well individuals can differentiate themselves within their families—or develop their own set of interests, beliefs, and coping styles—will influence strongly their level of adjustment.[7] Family factors including excessive Familyness (which is associated with family enmeshment, where everyone minds everyone else's business) or insufficient Familyness (which is associated with family disengagement, where no one cares much about other family members and distance is the norm), as discussed in this chapter, may reduce a family's effectiveness and diminish differentiation at the individual level. People with poorly differentiated selves tend to depend heavily on others' acceptance and approval, and seek to gain these through aligning themselves with others, bullying others into their point of view, or completely disconnecting from the family/group (as a means of avoiding rejection). In contrast, those with well-differentiated selves have more objective self-views, allowing them to weather interpersonal ambiguity, criticism, and rejection more effectively. It follows that well-differentiated people, who remain engaged with the family, and who can be seen as both products and promoters of optimal Familyness, will contribute most strongly to continuity planning by making decisions that balance individual and collective interests. Poorly differentiated family members will most likely avoid the continuity planning process or detract from it in various ways.

Promoting Optimal Familyness

Time and time again I have observed that families, who demonstrate interest and consideration for one another, spend quality time together regularly, and

---

[7] For more on Bowen's ideas related to differentiation and other family-based processes, see Roberta Gilbert, *The Eight Concepts of Bowen Theory* (Leading Systems Press, Lake Frederick, Virginia, 2006).

show real respect and regard for one another's views are the ones who are most successful with continuity planning—along with reaping many other rewards of the right level of Familyness.

Let's consider some of the specific, mutually reinforcing elements and processes that yield an optimal level of Familyness, which in turn serves as a key building block for wealth continuity planning.[8]

Fun

One of the simplest but most overlooked elements of Familyness is fun. Families that have a sense of fun and adventure almost always exhibit a good level of Familyness I see fun as both an output and input for Familyness. Such families demonstrate and build on their care for one another by sharing fun activities with goodwill and humor. The types of fun activities vary considerably. For example, one business family I know encourages its youngest generation to have their own outdoor adventures for members in their teen years and early 20s, including ski vacations, whitewater rafting trips, and participation in outdoor expedition-type programs such as Outward Bound and NOLS (National Outdoor Leadership School). The family tells me how energized the cousins are by the activities, and how they return from each activity feeling that they've gotten to know one another better, with enthusiasm for future get-togethers. That shared sense of fun and closeness dramatically improves the likelihood of designing and implementing successful continuity plans.

Given this, I encourage families to inject a greater sense of fun into contexts ranging from reunions to family meetings. Many family members dread family or shareholder meetings because they know they'll face boring agendas and technical details. They can combat this issue by thinking of fun ways to share information or take breaks, including having breakout sessions exclusively for the members of a given generation (this also helps people speak

---

[8] Not surprisingly, the elements that support a good level of Familyness tend to overlap with those that undergird other building blocks of the Foundation for Family Wealth Continuity. For example, storytelling will help to create both a sense of Familyness and strong Learning Capacity, as discussed in the earlier chapter on that topic. Rather than artificially relegating specific elements to specific building blocks, I have presented each element in any chapter to which it is relevant.

more candidly) or using some of the meeting time to share important historical or current stories that reflect the family's culture and values, as discussed next.

Storytelling

As discussed in the *Learning Capacity* chapter, stories are a highly effective way of promoting shared understanding within and between generations, which leads in turn to stronger Familyness. Many business families transmit their values, cultures, and practices using stories of previous and current generations. For example, I have worked with a century-old business family, a true tribe now, with hundreds of members dispersed worldwide. The family has a tradition of storytelling—grandparents and parents share stories of family history with younger members in both formal (shareholder meetings) and informal (family gatherings) settings, encouraging the younger generations to learn from these and apply what they learn to their own lives. Such practices create a better shared understanding of and appreciation for the family's history and membership, cementing a greater sense of Familyness for current and future generations.

Information-seeking/sharing

Having a shared foundation of information about the family and business can contribute to the right level of Familyness, as well. Continuity planning specifically requires a shared understanding of the family's assets, vision, and goals, at both collective and individual levels. As such, the families that plan most effectively have almost always created strong channels for information-sharing (this can also be related to the idea of Learning Capacity discussed in the previous chapter). That transparency contributes further to a sense of Familyness, as members feel valued by not being kept "in the dark" about key information that may affect their future, including information about assets and estate-planning.

Information-sharing, as suggested above, can take place at the individual and group levels. Individuals can be encouraged to discuss their future plans and aspirations, and these can be linked to continuity planning. Similarly, it's important to develop a sense of collective vision and goals—as related to a family foundation, for example—to further inform continuity planning and boost Familyness. Information about the business's performance, vision, and objectives is also critical. For example, many families invite key executives from the business—whether family members or not—to family assemblies or other events to present high-level overviews of the business for a broad group of family members (with more detailed information as needed); this promotes a deeper shared understanding that facilitates both Familyness and continuity planning.

Shared views and intimacy

Families that share views of themselves and the world will generally have a stronger sense of Familyness than those that don't. For example, an extended family that views itself as a true tribe will have stronger ties within and across nuclear families and generations. They will embrace the idea that there is strength in numbers (as long as there are connections among the members who make up those numbers). They will have a shared sense of justice and fairness. In such families, there may be little distinction between cousins and siblings—everyone is family, and everyone is treated with love and respect.

Such families will also tend to have a shared vision of the future and how to get to that vision. But note that the presence of a shared vision isn't sufficient for sustained Familyness. It's the *ongoing sharing* of that vision that creates the intimacy associated with Familyness. That means members have to be willing to talk regularly about their interests, hopes, objectives, and aspirations, including how these may change over time. Sharing in this way will enhance Familyness and further inform whatever plans may be in place. For example, if a family foundation board member has a life-changing experience after visiting a drought-stricken part of the world, sharing that experience with other family will enhance Familyness and may also have an impact on the foundation's future activity.

Earlier I noted that Familyness is a less intense emotion than what may be typically thought of as intimacy in other kinds of relationships (such as romance). That remains true, but there certainly seems to be an element of intimacy that is conveyed by the Familyness components of trust, shared vision, and other factors. In fact, a sense of intimacy may be jump-started by a simple exercise in which family members participate, as suggested by the "How to Jump-start Intimacy" box below.

How to Jump-start Intimacy

A 2015 *New York Times* article went viral because it described 36 questions two people can ask each other to increase the chances they would fall in love.[9] The questions were based on a 1997 psychology study designed to create "closeness in an experimental context" and included items such as these[10]:

- *Before making a telephone call, do you ever rehearse what you are going to say? Why?*
- *Is there something you have dreamed of doing for a long time? Why haven't you done it?*
- *Complete this sentence: "I wish I had someone with whom I could share..."*

People asked to share answers to those questions with a randomly assigned partner reported feeling much closer to the person than did those participants who were asked simply to make small talk with a partner (based on 36 non-intimacy-focused questions). The idea is that intimacy can be accelerated by mutual, meaningful sharing. In the same way, family members can heighten intimacy by asking and answering similar questions based on individual and family interests. Some questions that I find to be very useful for families who wish to participate in this kind of exercise include the following questions that I have gathered over the years through observation, discussions with family members, and interaction with other professionals:

1. *What is something about you that no one else knows that would help us get to know you better?*
2. *What keeps you up at night?*
3. *What is one question that you would like to ask someone else in the room? Ask it to that person now.*
4. *What is the most important gift you can give your children?*
5. *What is your best quality?*
6. *What issues have not been talked about openly, that should be talked about at some point?*

[9] Mandy Len Catron, "To Fall in Love with Anyone, Do This," *New York Times*, January 9, 2015, http://www.nytimes.com/2015/01/11/fashion/modern-love-to-fall-in-love-with-anyone-do-this.html?_r=0 (accessed May 19, 2015).

[10] Arthur Aron, Edward Melinat, Elaine Aron, Robert Vallone, Renee Bator, "The Experimental Generation of Interpersonal Closeness: A Procedure and Some Preliminary Findings," *Personality and Social Psychology Bulletin*, April 1997, vol. 23 no. 4, 363–377, (quote from p. 363).

7. *What gets you up in the morning?*
8. *Given the choice of anyone in the world, whom would you want as a dinner guest?*
9. *Would you like to be famous? In what way?*
10. *If you could change anything about the way you were raised, what would it be?*
11. *If you could wake up tomorrow having gained any one quality or ability, what would it be?*
12. *Is there something that you've dreamed of doing for a long time? Why haven't you done it?*
13. *What is the greatest accomplishment of your life?*
14. *What is your most treasured memory?*
15. *What is the most important achievement of your life?*
16. *What do you want your children to have that you didn't have?*
17. *What role did you play growing up relative to your siblings?*
18. *What is the single most important role you play in your family presently?*
19. *For what are you most grateful?*
20. *What is the most important gift you received from your parents?*

Sharing answers to these and other questions can help jump start a sense of intimacy that may help build Familyness in your family.

Altruism

Altruism, or putting someone else's needs ahead of your own, can be heroic actions such as running into a burning building to save a baby, but also occurs on a smaller-scale, including in families. Here, the idea is that when people are willing to sacrifice their own needs for the greater good, that will boost Familyness significantly. Altruism in this context can mean something as simple as prioritizing a family meeting over a much-anticipated round of golf.

But altruism can also represent a much more meaningful individual sacrifice. For example, in a US-based family business that sold automotive parts, only two of four siblings worked for the firm, rising eventually to become very successful co-CEOs. Based on their dedication and results, the parents and firm founders decided to pass along 100% of the business to them, splitting the family's other (substantial) assets equally among the other two siblings. Despite the parents' good intentions for ensuring longevity of the business *and* fairly sharing the family's wealth, their estate plan threatened to cause deep hurt and animosity among their children, as it was perceived as unfair by the siblings who were left without any ownership connection to a business that they had grown up with. That's not what happened, because the co-CEO siblings pushed for a more equitable arrangement: They decided to share interests in the business with their siblings. That created a strong sense of goodwill and Familyness that aided in both generations' continuity planning. It also added complications to estate and tax planning, but the family was willing to undertake those complications in order to preserve their relationships. Remember: It's rarely just about money; business families and families of wealth—and their advisors—routinely underestimate the value of intangibles such as fairness and harmony, sacrificing all-important Familyness in the process.

Good continuity plans—such as a succession plan that passes ownership exclusively to family members who are active in a family-owned business—may look good and proper on paper, but implementation may be deeply flawed if elements of the foundation that we have been describing are neglected. In this case, the succession plan violated the family's strong sense of Familyness and resulted in a disruption in family harmony, affecting the family CEOs' sense of justice, upsetting their relationships with siblings, and causing a chronic distraction to their management duties. It was, in turn, their commitment to the family that enabled the family to "reset the plan" and proceed in a much more productive manner.

Inclusiveness

Families with a high sense of Familyness are generally inclusive from early on. They seek out ways to welcome new members actively, including in-laws. Other families, in contrast, may consider *blood* as the only basis for family ties. This creates different "classes" of family members—direct descendants and in-laws—that may result in an us-versus-them mentality. Ironically, by trying to "protect" the family in this way, families who emphasize "blood" over non-blood may be undermining healthy Familyness and diminishing the odds of successfully implementing good continuity plans, as any such efforts could be accompanied by perceptions of injustice and inequality. While there are often legitimate reasons to pass ownership exclusively to direct descendants of a founder, families and their advisors should take note of the potential impact on Familyness. Open dialogue, transparency around the decision, and recognition and acknowledgement that a decision may seem unfair, are steps that could be taken to ameliorate negative impacts and that could in fact transform a challenge to Familyness into an opportunity for strengthening the same.

Families that embrace inclusiveness boost their sense of Familyness significantly, thus setting a stage for successful continuity planning. One family operated a family foundation that was intended to be an asset to all family members *and* a central point of togetherness and collaboration for generations to come. However, one young female third-generation family member avoided foundation meetings and was generally viewed as being distant and uncomfortable around family. Unbeknownst to the family, she had struggled for years with her sexual identity, finally accepting that she was gay, and she was highly reluctant to reveal this to the entire family, especially to her grandparents, who had always been religious and socially conservative. This dynamic kept her away from the family's operating company and from foundation activities and was a thorn in the side of many family members, potentially undermining the family's vision for the foundation and other wealth continuity structures. When, with the help of fellow third-generation members, she summoned the courage to share her "secret," she was pleasantly surprised that members across all generations accepted her with warmth and understanding. The experience affirmed the family's sense of caring and closeness not only for that particular member but for everyone, because it sent the strong message that "You are welcome here." Such messages form the bedrock of Familyness and make continuity planning—and in this case, a family foundation—much more likely to succeed as an inclusive wealth continuity structure. Inclusiveness may be promoted through some relatively simple undertakings such as:

- Developing an intentional program to ensure that different family members spend enough time together to assure unity and a common culture; this can be viewed as an opportunity for cross-cultural teaching and sharing
- Increasing the frequency of family meetings to close the "familiarity gap"
- Creating a simple newsletter—hard copy or online—through which members can share good news and other updates

"In-it-togetherness"
Beyond simple inclusiveness (discussed above) is a characteristic I think of as "in-it-togetherness," or the strong sense that a family will stick together when weathering new situations and challenges. Using a medical analogy: Early

studies of health-related compliance found that family support was critical for promoting good compliance with medical regimens. For example, compliance peaks when patients live with supportive family members, when multiple family members undergo the same treatment, or when family members take responsibility for some components of a relative's treatment regimen.[11]

In the same way, families that more naturally engage multiple family members in the development and implementation of a continuity plan will almost certainly drive better implementation outcomes. The sense of in-it-togetherness promotes better alignment and ownership of family members regarding the plan and results in increased goodwill and interest among members—all important contributors to and consequences of Familyness.

Warmth and comfort
The Yiddish word "haimish" refers to the sense of warmth, comfort, and familiarity people experience in a home-like setting. I saved this factor for last because all the other Familyness elements mentioned here can contribute to a sense of warmth and comfort that makes any process in a family—continuity planning and others—easier and more effective. But for too many families, the house is not a *home*, as they don't feel comfortable or supported when together. They may criticize or antagonize one another. Other families may not emanate warmth and comfort at all times, but generally provide the kind of support members need and thus enjoy an optimal level of Familyness.

The next section will help you assess the level of Familyness in your own family.

How Healthy Is Your Family's Sense of Familyness?

A method I have used to help family members gauge their sense of Familyness and to set goals for the kind of Familyness they would like, involves the graphic illustrated in Fig. 3.3. Imagine that all your relationships can be measured along a scale of intimacy ranging from 1 to 5.

The circles represent these different levels of intimacy:

1. Represents superficial contact with the world, such as brief contact with a stranger.

---

[11] See for example Robert Lowes, "Patient-centered Care for Better Patient Adherence," *Family Practice Management*, March 1998, 5(3), 46–57.

Levels of Intimacy

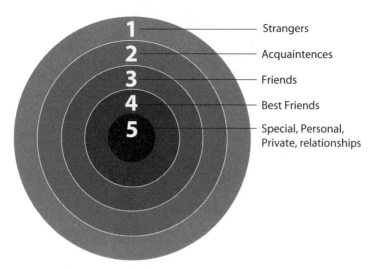

Fig. 3.3 Familyness and levels of intimacy

2. For people you would consider acquaintances.
3. For friends.
4. Represents relationships with one's closest friends and confidants.
5. For relationships in which you might share your most personal and private information—a very rare relationship, indeed, such as a good marriage.

On the scale of 1–5, how would you describe most of the family relationships you have with people in your family today? Are there any relationships that lie in the 4–5 range? Do any lie in the 1–2 range? Where would you like most of your family relationships to reside? Generally speaking, families who share relationships that are in the 3–4 range are doing quite well with regard to Familyness. Too many relationships in the 4–5 range may signal enmeshment and too much Familyness, whereas too many in the 1–2 range suggest a lack of familyness.

Along with the exercise above, answering the following questions may also help you understand whether your family's sense of familyness falls within a healthy range.

- Do interpersonal relationships within and across generations of your family feel unstable and tenuous much of the time? Do you often feel as though you are "walking on eggshells?"
- Is there a lack of caring and affection within the family?
- Do family members have low levels of presence, commitment, and engagement, leading to dissatisfaction at the individual and/or collective levels?
- Is your family characterized by an over-emphasis on spending time together, to the point that individual members may feel stifled or unable to express their interests and opinions? Does the expression of disagreement of any kind result in anger, tension, or discord?
- Is there a sense of "destructive entitlement" in the family: Does it seem that some members feel justified in mistreating others because they themselves or their nuclear families were wronged by the broader family in the past?
- Is there a sense that the family struggles to have fun together?
- Is a sense of intimacy lacking among family members, such that it is rare and difficult to share some level of emotion and trust with the others?
- Does the family tend to exclude members who may disagree with others or have different viewpoints or lifestyles?

Any "yes" answers to the questions above point out obstacles to developing a healthy level of Familyness within your family. The presence of many several "yes" answers may indicate a significant problem related to the development of healthy Familyness and warrants a much closer look at what your family can do to build this critical element of the Foundation for Family Wealth Continuity, using the ideas in this chapter and others.

Where Do You Stand?

In Fig. 3.4, place an X at the point along the column representing "Familyness" to indicate where you think your family stands with regard to the strength of your Familyness. A score of "0" represents non-existent Familyness, while 10 represents a very strong (healthy, not excessive) sense of Familyness. Your ratings on all building blocks (including those discussed in other chapters) will give you a sense of how strong your overall Foundation for Family Wealth Continuity is.

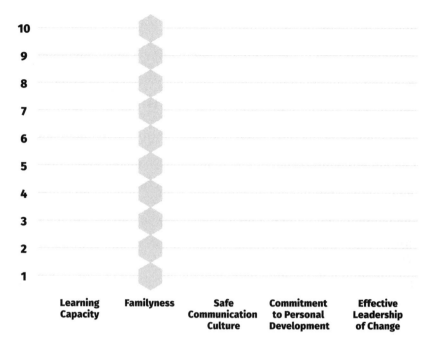

Fig. 3.4 Familyness: Your Rating

When Familyness Is Unlikely to Improve

As the earlier material in this chapter suggests, some families will struggle with developing a sufficient level of Familyness to conduct inclusive continuity planning effectively, or to care much about wealth continuity in the first place. For example, a family may be separated geographically due to educational or residential choices, or members of a blended family may have highly disparate interests and values.

When Familyness is unlikely to improve (as potentially suggested by a very low rating in the section above), it is sometimes advisable for the family to think of its members more as *shareholders* than collaborators. This makes a family business or family office more akin to a public company in which a wide range of individuals may hold shares, without relying on one another beyond that capacity. There is no shame in reaching the conclusion that this kind of arrangement is ideal.

In fact, there may be greater danger in trying to use continuity structures as a means of stimulating Familyness where little exists. That is, some families create a continuity structure to try to force greater collaboration and togetherness among family members. This was the case in one family in which the patriarch created a family office with the clearly stated intention of promoting harmony and keeping the family together by collectively investing family assets. While this plan kept the family's *assets* together, it did little to bring together a family that had rarely enjoyed one another's company in the past. Such efforts might include a plan to have regular family meetings, when a family has never had that tradition before. Or it may include setting up a family council to promote group decision-making, when every decision in the past has been made by a single person and no family member is prepared or interested in having that responsibility shared in a group.

The reality is that structures can *never* take the place of a genuine interest in collaboration. Structures can't provide the kind of emotional and interpersonal stability that comes with real Familyness. For this reason I encourage families to understand that not every family can or should aim to be a stable tribe. If you've tried to boost Familyness using the ideas in this book and others but it's not happening, then change the continuity plan to fit the family better, largely by promoting independent shareholding over deeper collaboration and decision-making.

Points to Remember

Here is a summary of key points from this chapter on Familyness.

- *Familyness* is reflected in family members' genuine interest in spending time together, including time related to their business and outside activities. Successfully implementing wealth continuity structures that engage family members requires this kind of stability, especially as extended families grow into tribes with numerous branches and cousins.

- Excessive or insufficient Familyness will hamper the implementation of continuity plans. Families that over-emphasize togetherness may stunt individual development and breed resentment related to the pursuit of individual interests and the expression of divergent opinions. Families lacking a sense of Familyness whether due to individual personalities, geographic dispersion, "entropy," or other issues—will also fail to provide a solid platform for individual development and sufficient focus on the common good.

- Among the factors promoting optimal Familyness are an emphasis on fun activities; storytelling; information-seeking/sharing; shared views that can be based in and/or promote intimacy; altruism; and inclusiveness.

- Families that may not be able to achieve a healthy level of intimacy may be best off thinking of members as shareholders rather than collaborators, and developing continuity plans in line with this mindset.

CHAPTER 4

Safe Communication Culture

D onald Chin didn't understand the problem. As founder of a $100 million California-based retail business that sold a wide range of cookware and kitchen gadgets, he had worked for years with a team of high-priced attorneys and accountants to ensure his five adult children—three sons and two daughters—would inherit ownership of the business in the most effective, tax-advantaged way. Even though only one of the second-generation members was likely to work in the business, Donald now in his late 60s, saw them as capable inheritors and owners, in part because several of them had strong business experience.

Yet, whenever he called a family meeting, it seemed some of his children did everything they could to avoid it, often claiming they were "too busy" with their jobs and/or family lives to attend. Moreover, whenever they did attend, the meetings tended to be difficult, with heated disagreements and a failure to reach consensus on much of anything, including the role that family members not active in the business could have as owners, and whether and which investment managers should be retained to manage the family's collective wealth. *Why is it so hard to help his children become good stewards of the family assets*, Donald wondered? As he neared retirement, the question loomed large in his mind.

Dee Chin, Donald's fourth child and younger daughter, could have told him why she hated the family meetings. In essence, they made her feel unimportant, and highlighted just how different each of the siblings was. Specifically, her oldest brother—who worked in the business—was clearly Dad's favorite and his opinions always seemed to matter most. Her older sister seemed uninvolved and disengaged, with two children of her own and a catering business to manage. The two brothers born just before and after Dee—a management consultant and physical therapist, respectively—were more willing to come to family meetings, but they disagreed with their father on many of the issues he presented. Dee believed this was because they had "something to prove," and had interests that diverged from her father's. For example, her youngest brother was adamant about devoting more of the family's resources to philanthropic causes involving environmental protection, which resulted in ongoing conflict with Dad.

Dee, an artist and writer, found the family meetings—and most any of their communications about business, succession, and estate planning—boring and overly complicated. While she understood the general importance of estate planning, valuation strategies, and investment options, she didn't want to get into the details of these matters several times a year, and felt she lacked the business/financial background to guide or sometimes even understand the related issues and decisions. What's more, her siblings with more business experience, especially her brother who worked in consulting, never hesitated to let her know she lacked such knowledge, whether they said something disparaging directly to her or simply exchanged knowing glances. Dee vacillated between wishing she could provide more input into the planning and being glad she couldn't, as she watched her siblings debate every aspect of every issue at the increasingly rare family meetings. For example, her brother the management consultant disagreed vehemently with her father and his lawyers about how best to approach tax planning, and each side seemed more interested in "winning" than in finding the best planning structures and solutions.

In general, the family's sense of goodwill and togetherness had been eroded by the ongoing avoidance and conflicts related to planning. Criticism had trumped caring in most of their relationships, and the family struggled to communicate not only about their continuity planning but about anything at all. Despite the business's on-going success and Donald's interest in ownership continuity, good stewardship, along with a real sense of Familyness began to seem more and more like a pipedream.

Scenarios like that of the Chin's play out in many families attempting to develop or implement wealth continuity structures. I have seen many instances of family members failing to understand estate plans, financial reports, or strategic plans. While a basic understanding of financial and other matters is absolutely essential to productive dialogue, the problem in the instance of the Chin family is compounded many times because family members across generations tend not to see or acknowledge the lack of understanding in themselves or others, they are reluctant to admit a lack of understanding, and they have not taken steps to develop a healthier communication environment that would enable safe self-disclosure as to their inadequate understanding.

The absence of an atmosphere that welcomes self-disclosure, vulnerability, and healthy debate makes it virtually impossible to exercise effective problem-solving and good decision-making when it comes to family wealth planning that is aimed at engaging and including the family while also preserving family assets. What is lacking is what I call a "Safe Communication Culture". That's the topic of this chapter.

What Is a Safe Communication Culture?

A Safe Communication Culture is the next building block in the foundation of family wealth continuity, as illustrated in Fig. 4.1. Even families that have strong elements of Learning Capacity and Familyness the building blocks discussed in the two previous chapters—may struggle to maintain a Safe Communication Culture, due to the personalities and dynamics of family members and their environments.

Culture may be defined as "how we do things around here," or the collective beliefs, behaviors, and actions within a family. As such, a Safe Communication Culture includes several interrelated features:

- *Family members are comfortable with honest and open dialogue*, without fear of backlash, criticism, judgment, or humiliation
- *Individuals demonstrate enthusiasm, or at least a willingness, to accept personal responsibility or at least their contribution* to difficult interpersonal processes, decisions, mistakes, or even outright failures (related to business and interpersonal issues) when they occur
- *Frequent, structured and unstructured opportunities are created for family members to talk to one another* directly and productively, including the ability to raise and discuss difficult issues without having any party or parties cut off or leave a conversation prematurely and without the threat that any party or parties may cut- off or leave a conversation prematurely

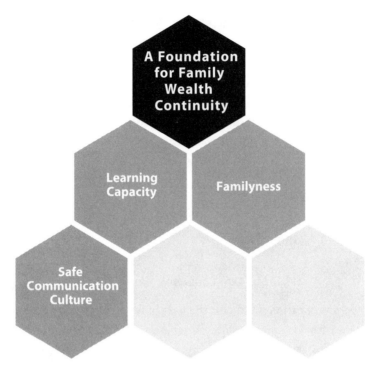

Fig. 4.1 Safe Communication Culture

- *Genuine caring and goodwill* among family members, who participate in these conversations—this is also part of the sense of Familyness discussed in the previous chapter
- *A commitment to reconciliation* when necessary, including a willingness to talk about past conflicts and perceived injustices with the goal of reaching better mutual understanding

A Safe Communication Culture is related to both building blocks discussed earlier: Learning Capacity and Familyness. Specifically, a Safe Communication Culture will enable the honest feedback and knowledge- transfer processes that are required for strong Learning Capacity; effective Learning Capacity then contributes to enhancing the communication culture, so the two building blocks work in concert, each supporting the other. Similarly, the goodwill and caring associated with a healthy level of Familyness will support a Safe Communication Culture, as noted above. At the same time, it should be noted that *excessive* Familyness when there is overinvestment in the family and members may be expected to give up their individual interests and pursuits for the family's sake—will leave little room for individual expression and interpersonal disagreement, resulting in an *unsafe* communication culture.

Earlier in the book I discussed the idea that some families represent *closed* systems, which are not open to growth or change. Excessive Familyness can create a closed system, as can chronic conflict and disagreement. A Safe Communication Culture is part of a more open system, one in which family members learn about themselves and others through honest interactions. Again, it's cyclical: A Safe Communication Culture promotes open, honest interactions, which in turn create an even safer culture for communication through a bi-directional process.

Don't Confuse "Peace" with "Harmony"

Safe Communication Culture means being able to have difficult conversations about important matters without a toxic impact on people or relationships. However, a Safe Communication Culture is not necessarily—and certainly not always—a "peaceful" culture. The patriarch of one family I know ceaselessly praised his children and their spouses for their cooperation with his plan for the family foundation, which included targeting one local charity with much of the family's charitable resources. "Peace and harmony," he would proudly declare when describing his family's engagement with his foundation's plans. Unfortunately, while there certainly was peace, there was little true harmony in the family. Seething beneath the surface were complaints and dissatisfactions with the philanthropic plan, the estate plan, and the terms of the various trusts that Dad had created. However, absence of a Safe Communication Culture, and the threat of Dad's anger, prevented any real communication from occurring in this family. As many families have unfortunately witnessed, when parental authority is gone—often upon a patriarch's passing—these dissatisfactions finally come to a head, with disastrous consequences. The absence of expressed conflict and dissatisfaction does not always indicate family harmony. It is difficult if not impossible to have true harmony without safe communication.

In this context it's important to note that the smooth operation of wealth continuity structures does not guarantee successful asset preservation *and* family engagement in the long term. In fact, as the example above illustrates, the smooth operation of these structures may conceal entrenched problems and may even work against family continuity, especially when the structures become *strictures* that limit communication. That is, if family members feel they have little opportunity to express themselves with regard to wealth planning, they may feel alienated, diminished, and disengaged, even while contributing to a plan's implementation. The plan, therefore, may not be sustainable for long.

Another way to understand this observation is that continuity structures typically evolve out of the dream of one person or a small number of people within a family, usually the founders or controlling generation.[1] When there is a lot of energy devoted to that dream—and when there are substantial sums of money or other assets at stake—it can be very difficult, and risky, for an individual to say, "Yes, but this is not my dream." Without the freedom to express oneself constructively and productively, well-thought-out plans may be undermined, actively or inactively, consciously or unconsciously, by those parties who are expected to engage with those plans.

On the other hand, if wealth creators become so focused on their own individual plans that they neglect, fail to consider the voice of, or ignore other participants—if a Safe Communication Culture is irrelevant to a wealth creator—then continuity may become a meaningless exercise, and family members may come to feel that they are irrelevant or even obstacles in a planning process. For example, in a recent meeting with a family, we had just taken a break from a discussion of estate plans that had third-generation family members receiving ownership in one of the family's operating businesses. The first-generation founder of the company and family office, a man in his late 80's took me aside and said, "We have to keep *them* [third generation] away from the active running of the company. They have never known what hard work means. *That's* why so many businesses fail." Moments later his granddaughter, a 30-something entrepreneur in her own right, collared me and whispered, "I heard what Grandpa said to you. I could never say this to him, but if that's what he thinks, why did he make us shareholders in the first place?"

---

[1] Several family business consultants and authors discuss in detail the "Dream" as a vision of the future for a family enterprise and the people within it, including the challenge of balancing and integrating individual and collective visions. Two good resources for this topic are: James Hughes, Susan Massenzio, and Keith Whitaker, *The Voice of the Rising Generation* (Bloomberg, New York, 2014) and Ivan Lansberg, *Succeeding Generations: Realizing the Dream of Families in Business* (Harvard Business Review Press, Boston, 1999).

This family was rife with conflict, dissatisfaction, and opposition that could be traced in large part to family members who felt they were subordinate to the family's wealth continuity structures and who understood that commenting on this situation would be viewed as a betrayal by the founder who was so deeply committed to the plans that he had made. In this way, wealth continuity structures can actually give rise to a communication culture that is unsafe.

As we have noted previously, wealth continuity structures themselves are insufficient to fulfill the goal of long-term wealth and family preservation; here we see that these structures are potentially destructive if they contribute to a communication culture that is perceived to be closed, even when it's ostensibly peaceful. Thus, families who seek long-term preservation of family assets and stability must work to create a culture or an atmosphere that enables and supports the difficult conversations that are sometimes required when family members are expected to work together and to make decisions together. These families will benefit from an environment that allows people to say, "When do I get my share (of the family wealth)?" and to ask specific questions such as "What does being a beneficiary mean specifically for me and when can I make investment decisions on my own?" or "Why did we make these specific investments and are they performing as they should?"

The Importance of Asking Why

Perhaps most important in the context of Safe Communication Culture is the capacity for family members to ask "Why" questions:

- "Why are we doing all of this in the first place?"
- "Why are we keeping our business in the family?"
- "Why is so much of our planning intended to maximize tax savings?"

Sometimes, "Why" questions are really intended as statements of disagreement: "Why are we doing this—it doesn't make sense" or "Why do you think we should keep the business in the family—that's a bad idea." "Why" questions posed in this manner are not really helpful and in fact may contribute to an *unsafe* communication culture, because they are fundamentally challenging and critical. But when "why" questions are posed within a Safe Communication Culture in an effort to really understand the purpose behind a set of actions, the questions can advance the planning and the family's engagement.

This is all the more true because wealth continuity structures are often developed based on "best practices," on the advice of advisors, or on "tradition," without clear, engaging explanations and understanding as to the fundamental reasoning involved. To take that point further, too many plans are developed without awareness of the needs, interests, and capabilities of the specific family in need and, not surprisingly, such plans, even those based on "best practices," are destined to fail without the better awareness and understanding an open culture of communication can foster. Thus when "Why" questions are asked and answered properly, there is an opportunity for family members to comprehend fully the basis of a plan that they are being expected to engage with *and* there is an opportunity for the plan to be adapted to the circumstances at hand. But the family culture must support the intention for family members to ask these questions and to expect meaningful responses. That is, it must be a Safe Communication Culture.

A good example of safe communication and the ability to ask "Why" occurred in a family who had sold a $100 million construction business in the Midwest and started a family foundation. The parents, the founders of the business, were assured that their children had received sufficient funds from the sale to be able to live comfortably the rest of their lives. Most of the founding generation's wealth would thus be contributed to the foundation. Their two children were apprehensive about challenging this decision, but believing that they could safely do so and have a good conversation, they asked "Why is so much of our wealth being funneled into the foundation?" "Because the foundation will provide an opportunity for us to work together as a family and to do good" replied the parents. "Why do you ask?" the parents continued, also trusting the family's respectful and open communication culture. Now, understanding that the foundation was being viewed as a sort of incubator of family relationships, the sons described their intention to start their own business that would also bring the family together while helping to nurture the sons' life goals as well. Based on this enhanced understanding, the parents, the sons, and their advisors then revised the family's plans for the foundation to provide additional support to the sons' new business.

Specifically, then, families benefit from a Safe Communication Culture in which family members may express individual and collective interests, discuss related hopes and plans for continuity, resolve conflicts and disagreements, and work toward reconciliation of interests, opinions, and personalities for mutual benefit, in both the short and long term. Wealth continuity structures are more likely to be sustainable and to be properly implemented within such a culture, as disagreements may be managed, collaboration enhanced, resistance mitigated, and other positive patterns nurtured.

It is worth repeating that by nurturing a Safe Communication Culture in which tough questions can be asked and answered, family members are not likely to feel secondary to the family wealth, as guests or intruders; instead they will feel essential and fundamental to a family's success. This is critical if a family's interest is in preserving both a family's financial assets and family engagement with those assets. As such, the "culture of questioning" should be all-encompassing: It can include questions about the wealth continuity plan and other critical issues within and across generations, including governance, family employment, succession, and others.

The following sections provide information on the specific factors that can promote or impede a Safe Communication Culture, and how to work towards improving them.

Trust as the Bedrock

Trust is the foundation of a Safe Communication Culture, a requirement for an environment in which family members can express themselves honestly and openly, without fear of retribution or resentment. In many families that I've observed that promote a Safe Communication Culture, trust exists at a most basic level: Family members assume the best of one another, and believe that individual needs will be taken into account by other members. Of course, that doesn't mean every interaction they have is positive or productive. That would be unrealistic and would be likely to prevent learning from experience. But it does mean that members of such families give one another the benefit of the doubt when it comes to motives, agendas, and reactions. That belief in mutual goodwill nurtures and cultivates further trust.

Psychologist Erik Erikson's famous stages of psycho-social development include "Trust vs. Mistrust" as the first crisis any human undergoes, occurring during infancy.[2] Specifically, infants enter the world uncertain of the kind of care they will receive, if any at all. If the infant receives consistent,

---

[2] Erik Erikson, I. H. Paul, and R. W. Gardner, *Psychological Issues* New York : (International Universities Press, 1959).

predictable care, it results in a sense of basic trust in the world and the people within it. Inconsistent, unpredictable care, in contrast, will yield mistrust in others. In the same way, it could be argued that every family develops a basic sense of collective trust or mistrust in its "infancy," based on members' early experience with one another, and that expectation continues on through the family's development. So a past pattern of trusting or untrusting relationships will be carried into the present and future.

In my experience working with a wide range of families, trust has been less a fixed, static quantity than a *dynamic* intra-family component. As circumstances and interactions within the family change, so does the level of trust. Consider two contrasting examples from family business. A second-generation US West Coast food services company is run by a brother (CEO) and several sisters (in other executive roles). They had made a good team for many years, with the understanding that each would reliably do what they saw as best for the business. There was no sense of hidden motives or agendas, with open, honest communication around business tactics and management styles. In other words, there was a strong basic trust. That changed when their children, the third generation, became old enough to join the business. Now the second generation became more guarded about their motives, seeking favor for their children in some instances, especially because there was a wide range of talent and acumen among third-generation members. As agenda-related suspicions grew, the family's sense of trust eroded, and it no longer felt safe to communicate honestly and openly. Any discussion of continuity plans—especially as related to leadership succession—became fertile ground for favoritism, conflicts, and hurt feelings. Only by relying on the board and outside advisors was the family able to regain a sense of trust and a safer communication culture.

At a different business, a third-generation family-owned retailer on the US East Coast, the oldest son of the oldest son in the second generation was a rising leader with something to prove (see my discussion of "Be My Clone Syndrome" in Chap. 2). Specifically, as he prepared to succeed to the CEO position, he took on a range of business and family responsibilities, including developing an ambitious expansion strategy for the firm and serving as head of the family council, a role in which he organized and rallied other members on important initiatives. Though they saw him as credible, committed, and competent, family members within and outside the business began to question the level of control the rising third-generation member had secured. In this case, the family was able to talk about the issue openly because they had a history of a Safe Communication Culture. Hearing the broader family's concerns, the CEO-to-be voluntarily stepped down from the family council leader post, communicating that it was best to separate leadership of the business and the family. The family embraced this solution, and the experience further strengthened a culture and environment promoting honesty and openness.

These two examples reflect the key components of an individual's trustworthiness, as discussed in the "Maister's Trust Equation" box below.

Maister's Trust Equation

David Maister and colleagues developed an equation that helps us understand why certain individuals earn more trust than others in a given group, including families.[3]

$T = (C + R + I)/S$

Where:

T is *Trustworthiness*

C is *Credibility* (Words), or what people say and how believable it is

R is *Reliability* (Actions), or how people act, in terms of their consistency across time and settings

I is *Intimacy* (Emotions), or how close people make others feel, based on the way they handle emotional issues

S is *Self-orientation* (Motives), or their perceived level of self-focus

So Credibility(C), Reliabilty(R), and Intimacy(I) all increase levels of trustworthiness, whereas self-orientation will diminish perceptions of trust, as illustrated by the two examples presented earlier. The equation can be applied to individuals but also to families, such that the more the overall levels of C, R, and I, the greater the trust—and the safer the communication environment.

While honesty is an important element of trust, I want to caution readers against pursuing the kind of "brutal honesty" some people may endorse— this means saying exactly what you feel, with no sugar-coating whatsoever.

---

[3] David Maister, Charles Green, and Rob Galford, *The Trusted Advisor* (Touchstone, New York, 2001).

While that may work in a minority of families, it can tend to promote a culture of unwarranted criticism and even contempt, one far afield from a Safe Communication Culture. Honesty should be based on support, caring, and compassion, with the intent to better relationships.

The idea, then, is to do what you can to build greater trust within the family, largely by boosting credibility, reliability, and intimacy among individuals, branches, generations, and other subsystems, as supported by caring and compassion. Addressing the elements presented in the following sections will help enhance this bedrock of a Safe Communication Culture.

The Shadow of the Unsaid

Everyone knows how damaging words can be in family relationships. But what's *not* said, or that which is left unspoken, can have a significant impact as well, including its relation to trust and the quality of the communication culture. Carl Jung characterized the unspoken and its consequences artfully in an essay he wrote in 1938[4]:

> *Everyone carries a Shadow, and the less it is embodied in the individual's conscious life, the blacker and denser it is. If (a problem) is conscious, one always has a chance to correct it. Furthermore, it is constantly in contact with other interests, so that it is continually subjected to modifications. But if it is repressed and isolated from consciousness, it never gets corrected and is liable to burst forth suddenly in a moment of unawareness. At all events, it forms an unconscious snag, thwarting our most well-meant intentions.*

In sum, what's unsaid—Jung emphasizes the unconscious element of the unspoken, but it applies to conscious, albeit unspoken, contents as well—can do more damage to families and the relationships they comprise than feelings or issues that are verbalized. The unspoken can "burst forth," as Jung suggests, to interfere with even the best of intentions. A family business example illuminates this idea further.

Gretel and her sister Tanya were at odds. They struggled to care for their terminally ill mother while comforting their grieving father and managing the financial services company their parents had gradually been transferring

---

[4] Carl G. Jung (1938). "Psychology and Religion." In CW 11: Psychology and Religion: West and East. p.131

them. But over the last month, any interaction between the sisters—phone calls, meetings, casual conversations in hospital waiting rooms—seemed fraught, with both Gretel and Tanya appearing frustrated, angry, defensive, or all of the above. This was a dramatic change from the goodwill and positive communication the sisters had always shared. If things continued the way they had been, the transition plan their parents had established—with Gretel and Tanya working together as co-owners of the business—was not going to be feasible.

Desperate for improvement, Gretel shared something important with Tanya while they waited in the hospital during their mother's chemotherapy session. "We've always been open with each other," Gretel said, "so I have to trust you with something I've been hiding." She went on to tell Tanya that their father had called her the previous month and made a dubious offer: He would loan her $1 million to pay off the mortgage on her home, with the unspoken agreement that she wouldn't have to repay him—an illegal plan to avoid taxes. Not wanting to confront her father during the difficult time the family was facing, Gretel had agreed to the plan, and to her father's request that she keep it from Tanya. Gretel told her sister that the plan had weighed heavily on her mind, and that, coupled with the stress of their situation, helped explain her anger and frustration in their interactions.

"You know what?" Tanya said after Gretel's confession. "He made me the *exact same* offer!" Now the sisters understood the root cause of their conflict: their father's misguided plan and request for secrecy. From that point the sisters were able to regain their mutual trust and goodwill, and used that to develop a plan to confront their father about the plan—they told him they would not take part in the plan unless he allowed them to actually repay the loans.

In this case, the father's plan had turned a formerly Safe Communication Culture into an unsafe one, by creating a large, damaging, unspoken issue between the sisters. Relying on mutual trust (discussed in a later section in this chapter) in the relationship, the two women had communicated openly to solve the problem and reclaim the safer culture, smoothing the path for resolution of subsequent continuity issues (such as how to handle their mother's share of the business after she passed).

I tell families who seek harmony in their relationships that silence *is* golden—but only sometimes. When secrets are kept about ownership and succession (such as a surprising choice as to the next family member CEO), when hidden agendas proliferate, or when feelings related to unfairness or mistreatment are unspoken, tensions and resentment will almost always accumulate until they burst forth in damaging ways. One way that family members avoid speaking their minds is through "triangulation," as discussed in the "Beware Triangulation" box below.

Beware Triangulation

Triangulation is a common mechanism of conflict avoidance in families. It occurs when two parties in conflict bring a third party into their issue rather than dealing with it themselves. So what should be a direct conversation becomes two separate discussions, with the disgruntled parties sharing their grievances with a third "point on the triangle." This can take many forms: a couple struggling to get along (or already separated or divorced) may talk about their problems with their oldest child (even if the child is not yet an adult herself); two conflicted siblings may communicate issues through a third; two family executives may discuss their problems with one another only with a trusted advisor, such as a non-family executive or board member. Regardless of the specifics, triangulation not only fails to resolve the core conflict, but also compounds the issue by inappropriately making others part of it and contributing to an increasingly Safe Communication Culture. The solution, of course, is for family members to be able to talk to one another directly—always easier said than done, especially in the context of historical tensions. Starting "small" and using outside advisors can help flatten the triangle into a direct line from one party to another.

The key, then, is to bring some of the unsaid out of the "shadows" and into the light—without dragging out *every* instance of negativity or hurt feelings (for some, silence is indeed best). I suggest that issues related to ongoing tension or that interfere significantly with continuity planning are best shared openly. The communication should not be intended as "therapy," but as a way to get past specific obstacles related to planning or other areas. A third-party facilitator may be of value, in part to place emphasis on listening and solution generation, rather than blaming. Positive experiences of this type contribute deeply to development of a Safe Communication Culture by helping family members trust that good communication will lead to a good outcome.

Turn Back the Four Horsemen

In seminal research on the factors most likely to predict divorce, researcher John Gottman identified what he called the "Four Horsemen of the Apocalypse"[5]:

- *Criticism*: Attacking your partner's character or personality, with greater focus on traits (like laziness) rather than behavior (like failing to clean up after oneself)
- *Contempt*: Undermining the other person's sense of self-worth through insults or expression of dislike, disrespect, or even hatred
- *Defensiveness*: Making excuses for one's behavior, often by attacking the other's behavior or "yes-butting" (as discussed in more detail in the *Learning Capacity* chapter)
- *Stonewalling*: Withdrawing from the relationship in a passive way, including physical withdrawal or giving the other person the "silent treatment"

In his bestselling book *Blink*, Malcolm Gladwell profiles Gottman's work and describes how the researcher became adept at understanding whether couples would stick together or split, longer term, by observing their conversations for as little as *three minutes* and looking for evidence of the Four Horsemen and other indicators![6] The findings suggest the big impact of small-scale interactions (which often reflect deeper problems within a couple or family). For the broader implications of small-scale positive and negative interactions, see the "Magic Ratio of Positive and Negative Moments" box.

The Magic Ratio of Positive and Negative Moments

Research has shown that we experience as many as 20,000 discrete "moments" every day, and that how good we feel about each day, and life in general, depends on how many of those moments we categorize, whether consciously or unconsciously, as positive—or, more specifically, the proportion of posi-

---

[5] For a description of the research on which the Four Horsemen is based and many other details from Gottman's work, see John Gottman, *Why Marriages Succeed or Fail* (Simon & Schuster, New York, 1995).
[6] Malcolm Gladwell, *Blink* (Little, Brown, and Company, New York, 2007).

tive to negative moments.[7] The magic ratio varies by setting and, probably, by person. For example, John Gottman's research (mentioned earlier) showed that a 5:1 ratio of positive to negative moments in a marriage predicted longevity; couples with a lower ratio were much more likely to get divorced. Other research shows that workgroups with a 3:1 positive-to-negative ratio outperform those with a lower one. But anything beyond 13:1 positive to negative is actually *detrimental* for teams, probably reflecting an inability to talk honestly about issues and conflicts. For our purposes, the idea is that a Safe Communication Culture depends in part on having more positive moments than negative moments, likely significantly more, without expecting that 100% of interactions will be positive.

Not surprisingly, criticism, contempt, defensiveness, and stonewalling make for a highly unsafe communication culture, whether they take place between individual family members or among groups within the family. In one family I knew, members were able to communicate about difficult issues only by email or handwritten notes, because phone conversations or in-person meetings inevitably devolved into criticism, blaming, and name-calling. This is a sadly familiar situation for many families. Of course, other families may not speak about anything difficult at all, to avoid negativity. Neither of those situations reflects a Safe Communication Culture.

Several tips apply to turning back the four horsemen of negative communication cultures, to promote safer environments:

- Rather than avoiding discussions of conflict or dissatisfaction (for fear that they will turn into criticism or contempt), set a *context of caring*: "I want to discuss this because I care about you and want to make sure we all feel good about each other."
- Rather than criticizing or expressing contempt, *describe your own feelings and needs using "I" statements*: "When you dismiss my ideas or act like I don't understand something, it makes me feel hurt and uninterested in taking part in family meetings."
- Rather than being defensive about your actions, *take responsibility* for at least part of a difficult situation: "I know that I tend to be dismissive at times in our family meetings, and I need to work on that."

[7] As discussed by multiple sources including Tom Rath and Donald O. Clifton, *How Full Is Your Bucket?* (Gallup Press, New York, 2004).

- Rather than passively stonewalling, *be actively honest*: "I think it's better for us to talk about difficult things than to avoid each other completely."

The Importance of Empathy

"I don't understand," the husband said, "she has everything she could possibly want, but she never seems happy." That's what the family CEO of a family office said about his spouse, when they were discussing her frustration about their relationship and current situation. On the surface, the husband's point seemed reasonable, as the family's investments were very successful, allowing the couple and their children to live an extravagant lifestyle including multiple homes and cars and exotic annual vacations. The wife had quit her job long ago, and enjoyed spending time with her children and friends, along with volunteering for several nonprofit organizations. But her frustration was valid: Her husband had taken control of all financial decision-making, including their estate planning. Whenever she tried to talk to him about including her input, she didn't get very far. So in reality she *didn't* have everything she wanted—she lacked a spouse who understood her point of view and who would be willing to take steps to address her concerns.

The problem in this scenario and similar ones is that one or more family members lack *empathy* for the others. Empathy, or the ability to put yourself in someone else's shoes and understand their feelings and concerns, is essential for a Safe Communication Culture because it enables a shared understanding that crosses lines related to personality, age, gender, generation, position within the family enterprise and within the family, experience, and other relevant dimensions.

While it's true that some people are more naturally empathetic than others—most of us can improve on this highly important dimension. One of the biggest steps to boosting your empathy is understanding and avoiding the "fundamental attribution error."[8] As complicated as it sounds, the main

---

[8] For more information (and a humorous take) on the fundamental attribution error, see Mark Sherman, "Why We Don't Give Each Other a Break," *Psychology Today*, June 20, 2014, https://www.psychologytoday.com/blog/real-men-dont-write-blogs/201406/why-we-dont-give-each-other-break (accessed June 19, 2015).

concept is simple: We tend to attribute other people's behavior, especially negative behaviors, to their personalities, while seeing our own as the result of our specific circumstances or situation. So the husband in the example above was attributing his wife's frustration to what he saw as a general tendency to be dissatisfied, when he should have taken her situation—inability to influence financial decisions—more into account. Building the question "What are all the reasons that family members could be acting that way?" into your analysis of other people's behavior, with an emphasis on situational factors, is a good way to enhance your sense of empathy for others and create a safer communication culture.

A strong sense of empathy is critical for successful conflict resolution, another key component of a Safe Communication Culture. The "Am I Part of the Conflict or the Resolution?" box below provides more detail on individual contributions to conflict resolution.

Am I Part of the Conflict or the Resolution?

Most every conflict among family members involves discrepant assumptions, feelings, and interpretations of events. The set of questions below, which I developed with my colleague Kent Rhodes, can help you think about your contribution to any conflict and its potential resolution.[9] Answering the questions honestly and understanding what they mean for your role in a conflict will go a long way toward reaching a resolution.

1. Can I identify any assumptions I have been holding that may be coloring my interpretation of events and conclusions I have drawn?

2. Have I made time to check out my own interpretation of information or events with other family members?

3. Have I made time to talk with other family members about those assumptions while working toward a better understanding?

4. How might I develop a more open-minded approach to simply better understand other family members' interpretation of the same data or events?

[9] Kent Rhodes and David Lansky, *Managing Conflict in the Family Business* (Palgrave Macmillan, New York, 2013).

5. Can I separate my feelings from what the other person may have intended?

6. Which of my own "buttons" is being pushed? Might I be reacting to personality differences or to events in the distant past?

7. Is my reaction in proportion to the conflict?

8. How might my attitude toward the problem or the person be influencing my perception?

9. How have I specifically contributed to the problem?

10. What specific actions can I take to (re)build trust between us?

Feedback Do's and Don'ts

A Safe Communication Culture is critical to successful implementation of wealth continuity structures, because in such a culture it is possible to discuss and solve problems that otherwise might undermine a plan or its implementation. In the highest-performing families I've observed—those who successfully engage family in wealth continuity structures and reap the benefits of those plans over generations—the provision of honest, constructive feedback is built into the family's culture. Importantly, communicating about difficult issues is a fundamental contribution to a Safe Communication Culture, because it promotes more honest communications and ultimately moves everyone toward a shared understanding of what matters at the individual and collective levels—in particular as related to wealth continuity planning.

There is an art to providing feedback well.[10] For example, people tend to react much more strongly to negative feedback than to positive feedback. In the workplace, overly harsh feedback undermines productivity. In the same way, feedback that is not provided well in a family wealth planning context may have an overall negative impact, reducing the likelihood that plans will be well-adapted or properly implemented to match a situation at hand.

So it's important to proceed carefully when offering feedback of any type. Below is some guidance for providing feedback in a Safe Communication Culture:

---

[10] Robert Pozen, "The Delicate Art of Giving Feedback," *Harvard Business Review*, March 28, 2013, https://hbr.org/2013/03/the-delicate-art-of-giving-fee (accessed June 23, 2015).

- *Understand the purpose of feedback*: In the context of wealth continuity planning, the objective of providing feedback is to ensure that a plan fits properly the circumstances and the people it is intended for. When people start using feedback as a source of power or retribution, the returns will diminish quickly and damage is much more likely.
- *Choose your battles*: Recognize that offering feedback, especially the negative variety, on too many things will result in a negative reaction. So aim to provide feedback on matters that are most important and that are likely to have the most impact on plans and the people who are being planned for.
- *Understand that not all feedback will have the outcome intended*: Offering feedback may be helpful; but understand it is an offer that may or may not be accepted. Preservation of a Safe Communication Culture will rest in part on reactions when feedback is not accepted.
- *Emphasize the constructive over the critical*: Public criticism can be one of the most damaging types of communication in a family, but family members routinely engage in it anyway. Be sure to provide feedback on plans, processes, and people in an environment that is supportive, such that the communication is not likely to be perceived as an instance of public shaming.
- *Manage emotional contagion:* Emotions are "contagious"—this is often most clearly manifested in the transmission of certain emotions from group leaders to group members.[11] It's important to remember this when providing feedback in a group: To the extent that the feedback is provided in a calm, clear manner, that emotional expression will likely be reflected in the group, helping to preserve a safe communication atmosphere.
- *Don't forget the positive*: Of course, it can be easy to focus only on negative feedback. As discussed earlier, a disproportion of positive communication will help to create and preserve a Safe Communication Culture.

It's important not to neglect the other side of the coin: *receiving* feedback. Specifically, receiving feedback can be an inherently threatening expe-

---

[11] For more on emotional contagion, see Daniel Goleman, Richard Boyatzis, and Annie McKee, *Primal Leadership* (Harvard Business Review Press, Boston, 2013).

rience, so it's important to understand the best way to do this.[12] Here are several tips:

- *Frame the experience as an opportunity:* In a Safe Communication Culture, family members are given the benefit of the doubt. In this case, that means understanding that feedback is being provided to enhance plans and to ensure that they will be properly and beneficially implemented.

- *Understand the basis of "intention/outcome discrepancy:"* While the intention of others may be to provide productive feedback, because most of us are imperfect in how we communicate, it is not unusual for feedback to be offered in a way that may seem hurtful or destructive. Providing the benefit of the doubt means accepting that although an outcome may be less than productive, the intention was a good one.

- *Focus on the relationship:* Feedback is more easily heard in the context of a positive, supportive relationship. In some cases, this will already exist. In others, feedback can serve as a means of building the relationship, as long as it is delivered and heard with shared understanding and respect. So focus on how the relationship can be strengthened by feedback, rather than dwelling on any rifts it might cause—that means being objective about the feedback but also honest about its effects.

- *Use "yes/and" rather than "yes/but":* Some people view feedback as an *opportunity for an argument*: They may hear the feedback provided, but their immediate reaction is "yes, but…." In one family, the leader of a family office was discussing his intention to include his children's interest in green investing in investment decisions. "Yes, but we discussed investing in some solar energy companies before and it never happened" replied one of his children. Beginning again, her father replied, "Well I never really understood how important that was to you." "Yes, but I tried over and over to tell you." You might get the sense that this conversation is likely to go nowhere—each time Dad tried to move ahead, his daughter "yes-butted" him. Imagine how this conversation might have been moved ahead had the daughter used "yes/and": "I plan to include green investing in our investment decisions." "Yes, and I have some ideas

---

[12] For more on how receiving feedback can be interpreted as a threat, see Ed Batista, "Make Getting Feedback Less Stressful," *Harvard Business Review*, August 8, 2014, https://hbr.org/2014/08/make-getting-feedback-less-stressful/ (accessed June 23, 2015). Tips on receiving feedback adapted partly from this article, as well.

for you…" "I never understood how important this was to you." "Yes, and I am so happy you know now!"

- *Encourage feedback:* As I mentioned above, families who are successful in implementing continuity plans and in engaging family members in implementing those plans, tend to have feedback-rich cultures. Asking for feedback can place it more under your control while contributing to a culture that encourages all forms of communication.

The "An Exercise in Safe Communication" box provides something you can use to promote a safe communication environment in your family or one you advise.

An Exercise in Safe Communication

Here is an exercise to illustrate and promote the value of a Safe Communication Culture. It can be conducted with as few as three or as many as 15 family members. Each member is given a fixed amount of time (5–20 minutes, depending on the participants' comfort with one another) to comment on or share their feelings about an issue of concern to the family. It could be about an estate plan that has been shared for the first time, or about distributions to family members from a trust, or about the family's communication and relationships.

The rules are simple:

1. You must speak from the heart.
2. No interruptions; everyone must listen until their turn to speak.
3. During your turn, you speak only for yourself, rather than responding to others.
4. If an individual runs out of things to say, the group can sit quietly until the next person's turn.

It's best if the exercise is facilitated by an objective third party who times each turn strictly. Though it may seem daunting to speak for the full time, most people are surprised by how much they have to say, and many mention they would have liked even more time!

The goal is simply to listen to one another. In doing so, family members have an opportunity to form a "container" for each other, one in which simply listening is sufficient and in which each person has an opportunity to share openly. That's a key feature of a truly Safe Communication Culture.

The Right Place for Every Voice

In the opening example I presented, Dee Chin struggled to find her place as a family shareholder, given her lack of business experience and interest (she was a technology journalist). The issue was compounded by her siblings' lack of empathy for her, which was often expressed as criticism. Not surprisingly, all of that contributed to a very unsafe communication culture in which it was nearly impossible to make progress toward shared continuity planning.

Part of creating a Safe Communication Culture means finding the right place for every voice. Many families make the mistake of assuming that the only voices worth hearing are those of members working in a family-owned business, or those who hold business or financial knowledge from outside training and experience. That family ultimately misses out on the potential contributions of individuals with more diverse experience. At worst, it creates a myopia that can support the kind of unsafe communication culture the Chin family experienced, which created ill will and distanced members from one another. Finding the right place, in contrast, makes members feel valued and more interested in participating in the continuity vision by making unique contributions to it.

Critical to finding the right place for every voice is *listening*. Observing the skills and interests of family members—non-defensively and without your own agenda in mind—can help you uncover their potential contributions. For example, if the Chin siblings had paid closer attention to Dee's abilities, they would have understood that her writing skills may have helped them develop a clearer vision for continuity, for example, by helping to write a document incorporating individual hopes and interests into a more collective vision for the family's future, not only as owners but also as philanthropists (her brother's causes, for example) and caring family members.

Finding the right place for every voice contributes deeply to a safer communication culture while helping the family identify the best way to integrate divergent interests, capabilities, and points of view.

How Safe Is Your Family's Communication Culture?

The following questions, based on this chapter's contents, can help you assess the level of safety of your family's communication culture, or that of one you advise.

- Is your family uncomfortable with honest, open dialogue?
- Is there a reluctance to ask "why" questions about continuity planning?
- Do family members repeatedly fail to give one another the benefit of the doubt or to trust one another's motives in general?
- Are there unspoken tensions related to wealth continuity planning, succession, or other important topics?
- Do family members prefer keeping silent over speaking up, for fear of how people might react to what they say?
- Is there a tendency for members to "triangulate" issues through third parties—whether family members or others—rather than dealing with them directly?
- Are family interactions marked by criticism, contempt, or defensiveness?
- Is there a lack of empathy within the family, such that members fail to place themselves in one another's shoes?
- Are family members afraid or unwilling to give or receive feedback about their behavior or impact on the family?
- Are there many family members who might be able to contribute to continuity planning or other matters but have no voice in these?

Any "yes" answers to the questions above point out obstacles to developing a Safe Communication Culture within your family. The presence of many "yes" answers indicates a significant problem related to the communication culture, and warrants a much closer look at what your family can do to build this critical element of the Foundation for Family Wealth Continuity, using the ideas in this chapter and others.

Where Do You Stand?

In Fig. 4.2, place an X at the point along the column representing "Safe Communication Culture" to indicate where you think your family stands with regard to strength on this building block, based in part on your answers to the questions in the previous section. A score of "0" represents a very unsafe communication culture, while 10 represents a very Safe Communication Culture. Your ratings on all building blocks (including those discussed in other chapters) will give you a sense of how strong your overall Foundation for Family Wealth Continuity is.

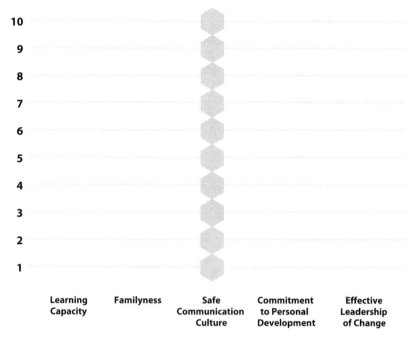

Fig. 4.2 Safe Communication Culture: Your Rating

So You Have a Safe Communication Culture—Now What?

Assume that you have what seems to be a genuinely Safe Communication Culture (based on your answers to the questions above), or at least that you understand the basic elements such a culture requires. What is it that should be communicated with reference to wealth continuity structures? Although this question may have as many answers as there are families who are contemplating family and wealth preservation, here are some examples of the types of conversations that can happen more easily in the context of a Safe Communication Culture.

- Ask "why" like you really mean it. Why are we planning to stay together for generations? Why are our trusts structured the way they are? Why is it best to remain as owners of this business?
- Share honest perspectives on the impact that a plan may have on individuals and on the family as a whole.
- Ask questions of the family's trusts and trustees: Are our trusts designed in such a way as to promote healthy family engagement? Are we being properly served by our trustees?

- Ask whether preservation of financial wealth is balanced appropriately with preserving family and family relationships.

Feel free to come up with additional questions or directions that fit your family's circumstances and goals.

What If the Communication Culture Can't Be Improved?

There is an interesting paradox related to the concept of a Safe Communication Culture: When it is possible to comment on *not* having safe communication, you are by definition taking a step toward such a culture, by discussing something difficult honestly and openly. In theory, observing and commenting on the need to nurture safe communication requires some degree of security and confidence that this will be heard, understood, and responded to. So the simple act of introducing this information to the family system may be the beginning of change. I am confident that safe communication can evolve in many (if not the vast majority of) well-intentioned families who consistently and persistently follow the suggestions outlined in this chapter. I've seen this happen many times.

Nevertheless, there will be times when this is simply not possible. So what happens when a family cannot develop or sustain a Safe Communication Culture, or when it may not even feel sufficiently safe to *comment* on the absence of safe communication? Consider the following example: Edward was the second-generation CEO and sole shareholder of a construction company with annual revenue approaching $1 billion. He had two children, now in their mid 30's, from his first marriage, and three children in their late teens from his current marriage. His older children had been involved in a nasty divorce and had been cut off from their father for many years. Only recently had they begun to restore their relationships, leading to both of the older children joining the company. The older children had also begun to develop relationships with Edward's new wife, Emily, and her children (their half-siblings).

All proceeded well until the family's first family meeting. Edward had planned to discuss the company's organization structure and the family foundation, which Emily now headed. No discussion of company ownership was planned. Unfortunately, Edward's oldest son did not know that. When he asked a question about future ownership, Edward, unprepared to discuss this, launched into a devastating barrage of criticism and anger, including the idea that his older children did not care about him or Emily. Emily joined in, and the meeting came to a screeching halt. Despite months of effort on the part of Edward's older children, Edward's estate attorney, and the company CFO, no additional meetings were scheduled and Edward and his older children became estranged once again.

This is clearly a family that had not developed a culture of safe communication. So what happened? When a family stubbornly fails to invite or support open communication, there is very likely a good reason that makes sense in the system as a whole. Introducing open communication in such a system might actually cause more *harm* than good. So what element of status quo might have been protected in Edward's family by shutting down safe communication? This became clear when I was asked by the family attorney for my advice. In the ensuing conversation I learned that Edward's estate plan ensured that Emily and her children would own 100% of the company's stock and that Edward's older children were completely cut out of ownership. So any effort to build "safe" communication in this situation could have led to a very "unsafe" outcome: revealing Edward's estate plan which would devastate his older children and destroy their relationships. So Edward chose a less direct path, not a very constructive one, but one that resulted in a gradual deterioration of relationships rather than wholesale destruction overnight. My advice? "Go slow. Edward and Emily are not ready for this discussion. They will need coaching and may need to revisit the ownership decision. The family will not benefit from open communication at this time."

Lacking a Safe Communication Culture is perhaps one of the best reasons to use an outside facilitator for wealth continuity planning, because a third party can intervene and provide perspective when the communication culture does not appear to be healthy and safe, as I did in the example above. A third party can also provide guidance to promote better listening and to ensure that feedback is offered constructively. But perhaps most important, an outside facilitator will know when to counsel a family to go- slow. A skilled outside facilitator will be able to advise the family to respect the internal logic of the system, to respect the existent family dynamics, and to accept that sometimes a gradual dissolution, coming apart, or soft landing is better than crashing and burning.

Points to Remember

Here are the key messages from this chapter on the Safe Communication Culture building block.

- A *Safe Communication Culture* within a family is marked by features including honest, open dialogue; a willingness to accept personal responsibility; and genuine caring and goodwill. Yet that doesn't mean that such a culture is always peaceful; rather, it promotes the ability to have difficult but productive conversations about negative issues and conflicts, including those related to wealth continuity planning.
- *Trust* is the foundation of a Safe Communication Culture, such that families assume the best of one another and support one another. I see trust not as a static collective family trait but a dynamic one that can shift based on time or circumstance.
- What's *unsaid* in families often has as much impact as spoken words, especially when resentment or misunderstandings are involved. Silence is not always golden, and families are encouraged to avoid secrets, especially about ownership and succession, as these erode the communication culture.
- The *"four horsemen"* that emerge from or predict unsafe communication cultures are criticism, contempt, defensiveness, and stonewalling. Families can avoid or diminish these by setting a context of caring, promoting "active" honesty, and having individual members own their feelings and contributions to conflict.
- *Empathy and feedback* are also critical to a Safe Communication Culture. Efforts to understand others' points of view can help promote empathy. Several tips apply to giving and receiving feedback, including choosing your battles, offering positive (not just negative) feedback, and understanding the difference between the intent and outcome of feedback.
- Families that find the *right place for every voice* are more likely to create a Safe Communication Culture. Members with a range of diverse experience and interests—not just business-related—may be able to contribute to continuity planning, given the opportunity.
- The presence of a Safe Communication Culture enables your family or one you advise to ask challenging "why" questions about continuity planning and its elements. If the communication culture *can't* be improved by the family, outside facilitators can be of value in continuity planning processes.

CHAPTER 5

Commitment to Personal Development

The leaders of the Vinson family office were puzzled by the survey findings: Almost every member of the cousin generation expressed minimal interest in annual family office meetings, which had been created in order for this generation of business- owners to understand the strategy and performance of the family business. The executives and directors were surprised there was so little interest in the operating company (which made components for large industrial machinery) that had generated so much of the family's wealth, including that of the cousins. They had initially suspected low interest due to the lacklustre attendance and participation at family office meetings, but the survey—the first of its kind for the family—confirmed the lack of interest.

As Vinson's leaders followed up the survey results with individual interviews of the cousins, they noticed a distinct pattern: It wasn't that the cousins had no *inherent* interest in the operating company, but more that the majority of them felt they simply couldn't understand the content of the family office meetings, from the company's financial statements and related ratios to the complexities of managing the trusts in which the family's wealth was held.

"I feel like I just don't get it," one cousin said. Another interviewee put it more bluntly: "Those meetings make me feel like a moron." Interestingly, the Vinson cousins themselves didn't realize how many of them felt the same way. They shared only partial responsibility for the situation: A lack of appropriate education and a failure to match the content of meetings to the cousins' capacity to understand it had contributed strongly to their feelings of humiliation and avoidance. Moreover, the Vinsons did not have regular family meetings that would have provided opportunities to appreciate and understand the dilemma they were facing, along with instilling a greater sense of the values underlying the business. There was no structure that promoted shared experience, values, and problem-solving, part of a more general lack of commitment to the kind of personal development critical for families that want to maintain wealth continuity.

This chapter is about Commitment to Personal Development as part of the Foundation for Family Wealth Continuity. The core idea we have discussed repeatedly is that wealth continuity structures cannot simply be "parachuted" into any family with the expectation that structures themselves—whether a family council, estate plan, or dynasty trust—will achieve the goals of maintaining wealth and preserving family. The foundational elements require hard work, and part of the effort must go towards promoting personal development, which ultimately increases individual and collective capacity to maintain and grow wealth and family harmony.

What Is Personal Development (and Why Does a Commitment to It Matter)?

Personal development is the next building block in a Foundation for Family Wealth Continuity, as illustrated in Fig. 5.1.

While the idea of personal development in general can encompass many facets, for our purposes, personal development refers to the effort, processes, and experiences that lead to the growth of skill, knowledge, and capacity of individual family members in the following areas (as illustrated in Fig. 5.2):

- *Financial and legal literacy*: A basic understanding and comfort with financial and legal structures, documents and concepts, such as profit and loss statements, trust documents, and stock and mutual fund reports.
- *Emotional intelligence*: An ability to understand and empathize with other people, the capacity to manage one's emotions constructively, and the ability to delay immediate gratification in the service of longer-term goals.
- *The Two H's: Health and Happiness*: A general sense of well-being, including facets related to physical health, mindfulness, self-efficacy, and generosity.

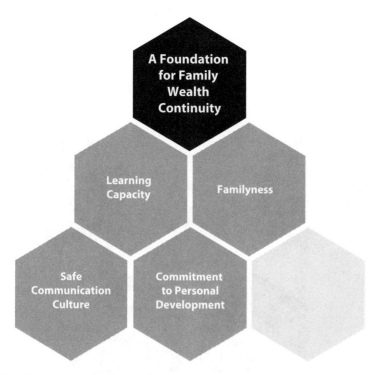

Fig. 5.1 Committment to Personal Development

These "facets" of personal development are critical to wealth continuity. But family members, wealth planners, estate planning attorneys, trustees, and others often underestimate the importance of personal development. Perhaps the best way to illustrate its importance is to consider family situations where a Commitment to Personal Development is minimal or absent. Families with a collective low emphasis on personal development are likely to be dominated by a minority of family members. Generally, these members, by virtue of their own hard work, or as recipients of the attention of others, identify with and hold competence in matters that are intimately tied to the family's fortune and future. This could be the wealth creator him or herself, a second-generation CEO, a family member who has attended law school and so on. This situation tends to concentrate power in the hands of a minority of individuals, with relatively little engagement by others. As Francis Bacon said, "Knowledge is power."[1] This is not to denigrate the accomplishments of these family members, but these family scenarios tend towards paternalistic cultures

[1] Sir Francis Bacon, Meditationes Sacræ. De Hæresibus. (1597)

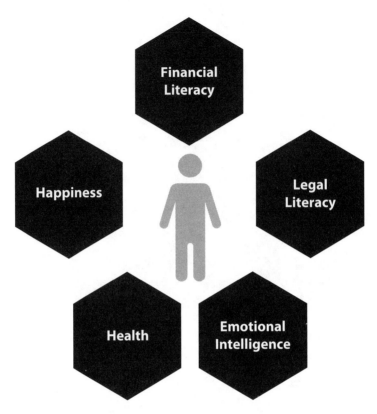

Fig. 5.2   The facets of personal development

in which decisions are made by a small minority. Now, this may be perfectly fine in some families, but if the goal is to create continuity structures that are inclusive and able to engage the broader family, a focus on the development of skill, knowledge, and capacity at the individual level will be essential to ensure that knowledge is shared by more than a minority. In short, without sufficient personal development among family members, wealth continuity structures are unlikely to be engaging to the family as a whole.

Consider for a moment everything that is required when families—particularly those with substantial financial assets—strive to create plans or structures that will engage family members, keeping family and assets productive and together.

- Capacity to *understand* the language that constitutes the plans
- Ability to *get along* with family members who are sharing the assets, the structures or the plans

- Ability to *share* tangible (such as financial assets) and intangible (such as history and values) resources and to *make decisions* with a spirit of generosity
- Ability to assume a *leadership role* in a family entity such as a family office
- Capacity to *understand* key features of an operating business, including financial statements
- Ability to *manage* complex service relationships, such as those with lawyers, non-family employees, trustees, accountants, and others
- Ability to *project* oneself into the future to understand individual and collective needs, along with the outcomes of decisions made in the present

Clearly, individual family members will need skills in several areas of personal development to do the entirety well. Consider three important overarching points.

Putting the "personal" in personal development
Many families I know make the mistake of seeing personal development primarily in terms of career or professional growth. While this is certainly important in the context of family wealth continuity, the kind of personal development that is most beneficial to the long-term interests of a family encompasses at least three domains: career, self-actualization (or growth of an individual toward highest-order needs, those that have to do with their deepest purpose in life),[2] and relationship aspirations. Wealth continuity structures work best when they serve people who benefit at a deep and meaningful level from wealth preservation efforts. In these circumstances and in these families, family members understand that to some degree the purpose of the family wealth is to enhance the lives of *individuals*. So I often remind families to put the *personal* back into personal development: To encourage family members to pursue growth experiences that may include career aspirations but may also include seeking internal peace, self–actualization, and growth in personal relationships.

---

[2] For more on self-actualization, see Ann Olson, "The Theory of Self-Actualization," *Psychology Today*, https://www.psychologytoday.com/blog/theory-and-psychopathology/201308/the-theory-self-actualization (accessed September 9, 2015).

Too often, wealthy families and business-owning families focus inordinately on enhancing and preserving financial assets while neglecting their human assets: family members. As noted earlier in the book, it sometimes seems that a family's money is accorded a seat at the decision table, and sometimes it's the *biggest* seat. And if we believe that people should be asking "why" questions (as noted in the chapter on Safe Communication Culture), such as "Why should we preserve our wealth for multiple generations?" then the answer better be something more than "because that's what the money wants!"

I recently sat with a 90-year-old matriarch and her 92-year-old husband, the founder of a publicly traded automotive parts company. The family was very wealthy, but their three children (now in their 50's) were extremely frustrated and unhappy with their parents, who insisted on ultra-conservative distribution policies and who sought to oversee the spending habits of two entire generations of family members—their children and grandchildren. "What do you want to see happen in the future of your family?" I asked. "Well," the matriarch responded, "We want this money to last for at least two generations beyond our grandchildren." "And what else?" I asked. "We would like to see the money stay together because that has given us many investment advantages," her husband replied. "Oh," I said, "and what about your family?" "Of course we would like them to stay together as well," he replied, as though this was an afterthought that required no further discussion. But without any further discussion this family would have been at risk of having very secure investment plans that seemed to have little connection to and little benefit for the family members. It certainly seemed that more thought and energy had been devoted to securing the future of the *money* than to securing the future of the family. That usually doesn't bode well for continuity.

Balancing individual and collective needs
While I heartily endorse the need to put the personal in personal development, as discussed above, I also encourage readers to seek a balance between individual and collective needs. Earlier in the book I described the idea that a Foundation for Family Wealth Continuity rests in part on balancing commitment to the group (the robustness of a family's Familyness with commitment to development of the self, as manifest in the pursuit of individual meaning.

As you might imagine, an overemphasis on either type of development will be problematic. When families exaggerate the need for Familyness (such as spending virtually all their free time together), this can stunt individual development and result in destructive resentment. On the other hand, an extreme focus on personal development at the expense of collective needs will undermine efforts to keep the family—and its assets—together. Understanding and applying the concepts in this book can help you strike the optimal balance between individual and collective development in the context of wealth continuity planning.

Commitment is critical

I have intentionally included the word "commitment" in this chapter's title. That's because it's more about the ongoing dedication a family and its members have to personal development—and to wealth continuity planning, in general—than about a given member's level of personal development at a given time. Very little that goes into continuity planning is "quick and dirty." It's about taking a long-term view, creating a vision of the future for the family and its assets, and putting a feasible plan in place to get there.

That, in turn, means being committed not only to preserving the family's assets but also to empowering the *beneficiaries* of those assets. And that brings us back to the central concept of personal development: If individual members of the rising generation are not properly prepared to receive the assets in ways that are productive and constructive, they will most likely fail to get the most out of the assets for themselves, the extended family, and broader society.

But where should the commitment lie? With the family as a whole? With individual family branches? With the nuclear families a branch comprises? Or perhaps only with individual family members? This very important question raises key issues that can only be answered on a case-by-case basis, since each family is unique. However, there are a few suggestions that should be considered as a commitment to the personal development evolution of a family:

- The family—or family entities such as a family council, executive committee, or key family leaders—can work to ensure that family members are aware of various personal development opportunities outside the family context, for example conferences and professional counselors who work with business families and families of wealth.
- The family or family entities can work directly to provide to the family, perhaps at regular family meetings, development opportunities such as those noted above.
- The family will need to decide whether and how development opportunities will be paid for by the family at large, by smaller family units, or by individuals. Many families I know view these opportunities as

essential for the health of the family and willingly underwrite expenses. Other families will request a report from the attending family member in exchange for underwriting the expenses.

- In combination with various considerations noted above, some families, while recognizing that development cannot be imposed on individuals, can require certain development experiences on the part of individuals *before* they partake in certain family initiatives. For example, membership on a family council may require prior attendance at family business or family office conferences.

- Finally, personal development is indeed personal. The final authority on this matter is each individual family member; and each family member, drawing from resources available within and offered by the family will need to provide the energy, initiative, and personal commitment that will be ultimately required of any effort in this matter.

Let's turn now to understanding each of the areas that make up personal development.

Financial and Legal Literacy

I've included financial and legal matters first here, not because it's the most important facet of personal development, but because it's a more circumscribed dimension to consider, and one that families often overlook. In fact, a lack of basic financial capability and familiarity with legal documents may be mistaken for much more complex sources of disruption to continuity planning. Specifically, when wealth continuity structures fail to be implemented, or when rising-generation family members are seen as disengaged or overly extravagant with money, or when discord mounts about continuity planning decisions, many families assume that personalities or interpersonal problems are the root cause. They may fail to understand that often a simple lack of financial or legal knowledge is at play.

For example, in one family, the 40-something CEO of an operating company was persistently frustrated with his two younger brothers who had careers outside the family business and who seemed disengaged from the operating company that they would eventually own together. At a family meeting the CEO expressed his frustration, including spouting off several theories about their detachment: His two brothers resented him because of his position in the business, or they were angry at the business because of the time it took from their family life growing up, or their wives were the cause of their disengagement. "Not the case at all!" the youngest brother exploded. "If you tried for even one minute to *explain* anything you presented, we'd be happy to attend your meetings."

Building Financial Literacy

There is consensus within and outside the family business and family wealth domains that financial literacy should start early, even in childhood. For example, Harvard's former senior philanthropic advisor Charles Collier suggests that children as young as eight should be given an allowance as a financial education tool (helping them set a budget, save, and spend carefully), along with being asked to help the family decide what causes to donate money to.[3] Subsequent activities can include helping teenagers manage spending and credit card use, along with teaching the basics of investment accounts such as brokerage and retirement funds. Collier's overarching advice is for parents to be open and honest about financial matters with their children, rather than creating a sense of secrecy around these. I heartily endorse this approach for business families and families of wealth. See the "10 Financial Skills to Master by Adulthood" box below for more guidelines on this topic.

10 Financial Skills to Master by Adulthood

Financial literacy expert Joline Godfrey suggests that everyone should gain capability in these basic skills by age 18[4]:

1. How to save.
2. How to keep track of money.
3. How to get paid what you're worth.
4. How to spend wisely.
5. How to talk about money.
6. How to live on a budget.
7. How to invest.
8. How to exercise an entrepreneurial spirit.
9. How to handle credit.
10. How to use money to change the world.

[3] "Raising Financially Responsible Children: A Conversation with Charles W. Collier," Merrill Lynch Private Banking and Investment Group Whitepaper, Volume 4, Fall 2004.
[4] Joline Godfrey, *Raising Financially Fit Kids* (Ten Speed Press, New York, 2013).

There are many resources available to help build financial skills at any age. Here are several that I have found of value:

Books
- *Wealth: Grow It and Protect It* by Stuart E. Lucas (FT Press, 2012)
- *Silver Spoon Kids. How Successful Parents Raise Responsible Children* by Eileen Gallo and Jon Gallo (McGraw-Hill, 2002)
- *Family Business by the Numbers: How Financial Statements Impact Your Business* by Norbert E. Schwarz (Palgrave Macmillan, 2010)
- *Raising Financially Fit Kids* by Joline Godfrey (Ten Speed Press, 2013)

Financial Consultancies
- The Redwoods Initiative (www.redwoodsinitiative.com)
- Independent Means (www.independentmeans.com)

A Comprehensive Approach to Financial and Legal Literacy

An effective approach to building financial and legal literacy will have multiple mutually reinforcing components. Here are some of the general steps I recommend to build such knowledge and capability within your family or in one you advise:

- Review the documents—including all financial and legal elements—carefully with financial planners and attorneys, encouraging questions
- Provide extensive learning aids (books, online resources) that are adapted strategically to individuals' learning styles
- Create a culture where people don't feel ashamed to ask for repeated clarification about financial/legal concepts and plans (see below for more)
- Provide formal training in financial and legal literacy, such as a workshop run by a financial/investment or legal expert
- Engage the rising generation as early (in their late teens at latest) and as much as possible, in planning and implementing related educational programs

A No-Stupid-Questions Culture

Through experience I've learned to ask a simple question of wealthy families who have done some continuity planning: "Have you read the trusts and do you understand them?" That may seem like a silly question to ask when so much is at stake, but I've learned how important it is to pose that query for multiple reasons:

- In many cases, family members haven't actually read the documents carefully if at all.
- Even if they have read the documents, many, if not most, family members don't understand them sufficiently.
- Of those who don't understand the documents, the majority don't want to ask any questions about them because they don't want to appear ignorant.
- Even the people hired to manage the various plans and structures involved—financial planners, attorneys, and others—often don't recognize the full extent of family members' lack of understanding, or how to address this effectively.

Given this state of affairs, and the need for inheritors to understand documents in order to engage with them and implement them properly, a family needs to pay close attention to its culture: In many families, there is a fear of asking stupid questions, especially when it comes to money or legal matters—as suggested above. The remedy is the encouragement of a culture that promotes openness and accommodates any questions, no matter how "stupid" the questioner may think they are. Family meetings are good forums for encouraging questions, but the best cultures in this respect provide a safe space for questions in any context.

Emotional Intelligence

I can't over-emphasize the importance of "emotional intelligence" in the context of family wealth continuity structures that are intended to engage family members over the long term. If members handle emotional and interpersonal issues skillfully and insightfully, a whole host of conflicts, misunderstandings, and obstacles to individual and collective well-being can be avoided, including those related to continuity planning.

What Is Emotional Intelligence?

Rather than representing a single quality or unitary concept, emotional intelligence comprises several mutually reinforcing components in individuals, including[5]:

[5] For much more on the components of emotional intelligence and their features and functions, see Daniel Goleman, *Emotional Intelligence: Why It Can Matter More Than IQ* (Bantam Books, New York, 2005) and Daniel Goleman, "What Makes a Leader?" *Harvard Business Review*, January, 2004, https://hbr.org/2004/01/what-makes-a-leader (accessed July 28, 2015).

- *Self-awareness*: Your ability to recognize your emotions and how they affect others—related closely to a sense of confidence and/or realistic self-assessment.
- *Self-regulation*: Your ability to control disruptive emotions and suspend judgment, as suggested by openness to change and other traits.
- *Empathy*: Your ability to place yourself in others' shoes and understand their emotional issues and responses, as suggested by skill in developing relationships across multiple dimensions.
- *Social skill*: Your competence in finding common ground, building goodwill, and managing relationships as part of a broader network.

Taken individually or collectively, these qualities could be critical to a family's ability to keep family and assets together for the long term. For example, rivaling siblings in a family business will fail to recognize their self-focus in the first place (due to a lack of *self-awareness*) and won't understand its negative impact on others (due to a lack of *empathy*), potentially leading to dissension and broken agreements, including those related to continuity plans. And of course *social skill* is a must for any complex, potentially conflict-generating group activity such as continuity planning, where strong communication and sensitivity breed success.

Emotional intelligence in the context of continuity planning rests in part on another quality required for success with this endeavor: delay of gratification. It's not hard to see that the inability to delay gratification could result in over-consumption of family assets (such as inordinate spending on luxury items, or unquenched desire for distributions and liquidity, rather than a long-term investment horizon).

Delay of gratification refers as well to an ability to restrain from immediate reactions, that is, to think before acting and thus to avoid acting impulsively. This is a personal quality that contributes significantly to conflict resolution and to problem-solving, activities that are key ingredients of any effort to enhance family collaboration and cooperation.

The Power of Empathy

While most elements of emotional intelligence will contribute to successful wealth continuity planning that engages family members properly, I want to draw particular attention to the power of *empathy*, or the ability to place oneself in another's shoes, whether you are a family leader, family employee/

owner, or advisor to a wealthy family. Consider a common scenario: From a founder's perspective it is not unusual for a leadership succession plan to be put in place, but for the plan to be the source of family trauma because the founder continues for years, even decades, to be a very active contributor to the business, coming to board meetings and questioning decisions about strategy, operations, and hiring, though no longer in any formal role. In such cases, the founder may fail to understand, to empathize, with his/her successors, not comprehending the negative impact on their commitment to the business.

The lack of empathy can extend easily to other continuity planning issues and decisions. A colleague of mine and I have discussed what we call "latent development syndrome," or a situation in which adult inheritors live lives of frustrated helplessness because wealth creators and family office executives failed to empathize with their need to have some control over their inheritance.[6] In such scenarios, we have helped founders, other senior family members, and family office and family business executives, step back from day-to-day control to give members of the rising generations breathing- room and space for decision-making. In part this is done by asking people to put themselves in others' shoes. A little empathy goes a long way.

The *Safe Communication Culture* chapter discusses empathy in detail, including means of improving your capacity for empathizing with others. As with the delay of gratification concept discussed earlier, empathy probably has an innate component but is not fixed in place. A recent *New York Times* article, for example, is titled, "Empathy is Actually a Choice."[7] The authors describe how empathy is influenced by many factors—you are more likely to feel more empathy toward members of your own country or race, for instance, as suggested by multiple studies. Moreover, empathy can be seen as a limited resource: You only have so much empathy to give. At the same time, we can shift the focus and/or limits of our empathy. For example, a recent study showed that just hearing the idea that empathy could be

[6] David Lansky and Anne Hargrave, "The Family Office: How to Avoid 'Latent Development Syndrome,'" *The Family Business Advisor*, http://www.thefbcg.com/the-family-office-how-to-avoid-latent-development-syndrome/ (accessed October 30, 2015).
[7] Daryl Cameron, Michael Inzlicht, and William Cunningham, "Empathy is Actually a Choice," July 10, 2015, http://www.nytimes.com/2015/07/12/opinion/sunday/empathy-is-actually-a-choice.html?_r=0%201/4 (accessed July 29, 2015).

improved was enough to enhance people's empathy for those outside of their racial group.[8]

In short, as the authors of the article noted above point out, "empathy is only as limited as we choose it to be." That means family members can move willingly toward being more empathic toward one another, particularly as related to issues around continuity planning—who should be involved, what kinds of structures and processes will be most beneficial to whom, and how others are affected and react to plans and structures that are put in place. Thinking about these items from others' points of view will make for much more engaging and effective planning.

Specific steps toward enhancing empathy may include:

- *Ask questions*: As simple as it sounds, asking questions of other family members is the easiest way to understand what they are thinking or feeling. How do they feel about a specific issue or event? What do they think is the best course forward and why? To enhance your empathy, ask questions like these and listen carefully to the answers.

- *Use your imagination*: Along with asking questions, you can mentally place yourself in others' shoes by imagining what they must be feeling and thinking about a given situation. In this case, it's about asking *yourself* questions to stimulate your imagination: How does this situation or decision affect the other person? What must they be feeling about it? How will they feel about my actions or decisions related to it?

- *Look beyond business and money*: In business families and families of wealth it is easy for family members to focus exclusively on business and financial issues. That's a mistake, because much of what people react to lies outside these domains. Boost your empathy by thinking about how other family members might be feeling about items such as responsibilities (within the family business or family office, for example), recognition, and how well their interests align with what they do for the firm/family.

---

[8] Karina Schumann, Jamil Zaki, and Carol Dweck, "Addressing the Empathy Deficit: Beliefs about the Malleability of Empathy Predict Effortful Responses when Empathy is Challenging," *Journal of Personality and Social Psychology*, Vol. 107(3), Sep 2014, 475–493.

Improving Emotional Intelligence

Just as empathy can be enhanced, so too can emotional intelligence. Historically, this was not generally believed to be the case, in part because the source of emotional intelligence was viewed as lying in the more primitive parts of the brain—including the limbic system—regions responsible for deeply ingrained, instinctual responses such as fight or flight. But recent evidence suggests that emotional intelligence and more general intelligence overlap neurologically more than previously thought, with some localization in the frontal cortex and other more "advanced" parts of the brain.[9] That means emotional intelligence may be more easily acquired or enhanced than once believed.

So how does one improve emotional intelligence? One way to lay the groundwork for improvement in this area is to follow the advice provided in earlier chapters of this book, advice that is aimed at the broader family culture. Establishing good *Learning Capacity* within a family will ensure that some measures that concomitantly improve emotional intelligence (such as asking questions of others) are integrated and potentially institutionalized within the broader family. Further, maintaining a healthy sense of *Familyness* will help to ensure high levels of empathy and will help to sustain delayed gratification in relationships and thoughtful, non-impulsive interpersonal interactions. Finally, a *Safe Communication Culture* will not only support candor regarding how people treat one another, but also ensure ample opportunities to provide and receive feedback, as discussed at length in the earlier chapter on that topic.

Harvard researcher Daniel Goleman, who pioneered much of the thinking on emotional intelligence, talks about the pliability of this resource, and how both nature and nurture play important roles.[10] For example, he notes that emotional intelligence increases with age, as part of the process of gaining maturity. Effective approaches on an individual learning level take a *behav-*

[9] "Scientists Complete First Map of Emotional Intelligence in the Brain," *US News and World Report*, January 28, 2013, http://health.usnews.com/health-news/news/articles/2013/01/28/scientists-complete-1st-map-of-emotional-intelligence-in-the-brain (accessed July 29, 2015).

[10] Material in this section from Daniel Goleman, *Emotional Intelligence: Why It Can Matter More Than IQ* (Bantam Books, New York, 2005) and Daniel Goleman, "What Makes a Leader?" *Harvard Business Review*, January, 2004, https://hbr.org/2004/01/what-makes-a-leader (accessed July 28, 2015).

ioral approach, one that relies on breaking negative habits related to emotional intelligence and establishing new ones. For example, Goleman provides the example of an executive seen as un-empathic by colleagues: a poor listener who interrupted colleagues routinely. To approach the problem, the executive would need to commit to improvement, be willing to have others point out instances where she fails to listen or interrupts, and then "replay" the incident with a more effective response on her part. Similarly, she could learn by shadowing peers who exemplify emotional intelligence, learning by observing and mimicking them.

Thus the key steps to improving emotional intelligence include:

- A *commitment* to enhancing this ability
- A willingness to have others observe you and provide *feedback* on areas that require improvement (or even videotaping your interactions to look for such areas)
- *Practice* of more effective social responses on the multiple dimensions of social intelligence
- The enlistment of a *coach* to provide more formal instruction and feedback

It's important to remember that trying new ways of behaving may feel unnatural at first, or uncomfortable at the very least. But the important thing is to stick with it. More and more evidence suggests that behavior can lead to internal change from the *outside-in*. For example, smiling, even when you don't feel like smiling, makes you feel happier.[11] In the same way, behaving in a more emotionally intelligent way can result in greater understanding of how to interact with others effectively.

As noted earlier, whether a family will provide this type of training to its members and what kind of training should be provided can be addressed on a case-by-case basis. I have worked with several families—both families with operating businesses and those with a family office—who decided that the benefits of a family-wide program in this respect far outweighed the relatively modest investment required.

---

[11] See for example Melinda Wenner, "Smile! It Could Make You Happier," *Scientific American*, August 1, 2009, http://www.scientificamerican.com/article/smile-it-could-make-you-happier/ (accessed July 29, 2015).

The Two H's: Health and Happiness

Last but certainly not least, the overall levels of health and happiness in a family—which are of course related—will promote effective, engaged continuity planning.

This is critical: We tend to take health and happiness for granted, but if even a *single* family member is struggling or has chronic health or mental health issues, it can derail not only wealth continuity structures but the entire family. I have seen this not only as a family business consultant but as a clinical psychologist.

For example, I worked with one family intent on creating a shared ownership structure in the second generation of the business. Dad was the founder of a successful pharmaceutical company, his son was the second-generation CEO and two daughters were interested, though not active, owners. A second son, the youngest child, had a history of addiction and mental health problems. The goal was to create an effective, inclusive second-generation ownership group. Mom and Dad insisted that all their children be involved in the ownership group. They did everything right: Stressed the importance of Learning Capacity and safe communication, provided educational opportunities, strived to spend quality time together. But it was all to no avail. The youngest son's mental health problems became a focus of every family meeting, and resulted in factions within the sibling group: two of the siblings thought their youngest brother should be forced out of the ownership group, while the other insisted, along with the parents, that he be included every step of the way. This dilemma not only destroyed the well-intended ownership succession plan, but damaged family relationships as well.

In another family I worked with, the first-generation founder of an automobile retail business would not sign his estate plan, which stipulated a significant amount of wealth to be transferred to his three children, until he could be sure that his oldest daughter was "cured" of her chronic depression. He didn't want to burden her with the details until she was recovered. Needless to say, he had to be disavowed of the view that it was wise to wait until she was "cured" of a truly chronic condition. Both of these examples illustrate the challenge of developing and implementing inclusive wealth continuity structures and plans, when some family members are clearly suffering and struggling to adapt or contribute.

A family that is striving to be truly inclusive as to continuity plans and structures faces a paradox: How to be inclusive and engaging without being imposing. This is particularly apparent when it comes to the subject of health and happiness. Again, while personal health and happiness are fundamentally related to the success of long-term continuity plans, it is simply not possible or advisable to impose a *standard* of health or happiness on family members. Therefore, the options for families seem to include the following:

1. Families can bring to the collective awareness of their members *external opportunities* such as speakers, workshops and conferences, to enhance lifestyle, mood and health.
2. Families can introduce programs to *family meetings* that address these issues.
3. Families can seek *expert advice* on how best to address individual challenges when these challenges attract family attention, energy and concern.
4. Most importantly, families can strive to *reduce and eliminate stigma* and encourage *open dialogue* in appropriate forums about health and happiness issues.
5. Ultimately each individual needs to be encouraged to take *personal responsibility* for managing these quality-of-life issues.

Below are what I consider the core elements of health and happiness. I'll keep it brief, as most people intuitively understand what goes into health and happiness—actually putting it into practice is the hard part.

- *Physical health*: Let's face it: If you have a bad toothache, nearly everything else matters very little to you in the moment, let alone much more life-threatening diagnoses such as cancer. There's a reason that physiological needs occupy the first level of Maslow's well-known hierarchy of human needs.[12] Still, many of us don't commit to our physical health in a meaningful way. This doesn't have to mean becoming a fitness nut or bodybuilder, but an effective approach could center on committing to a healthier lifestyle and understanding that includes diet, exercise, and the pursuit of fulfilling activities and relationships.

[12] Abraham Maslow, "A theory of human motivation," *Psychological Review*, 1943, 50 (4) 370–96.

- *Optimism*: There is increasing evidence that a positive outlook on life is linked to more effective functioning in professional and personal domains. Renowned psychologist Martin Seligman, for example, has integrated 25 years of human and animal research to confirm the power of optimism and the danger of pessimism.[13] For example, pessimists tend to feel "learned helplessness" (that nothing they do will change their outcomes) whereas optimists see problems as temporary and solvable. Applied to continuity planning, optimism can help family members become more effective problem-solvers and more likely to sustain hope when facing challenges that threaten to disrupt plans or structures. Seligman and others present many ways to become more optimistic, including taking time to feel grateful, as discussed next.
- *Gratitude*: The happiest, most mature people tend to feel a deep sense of gratitude or thankfulness for the things in their lives. They don't take things for granted, they are able to live in the moment, and take the time to think about what they value most in their lives. I believe firmly that not only a sense of gratitude but also its expression are critical to happiness—and effective, inclusive continuity structures. Gratitude can help make continuity planning more about the collective good, reducing a focus on self-interest, engaging family members to support plans and structures that benefit all, and encouraging greater interest in charitable works and philanthropy.
- *Generosity*: Generosity is closely related to gratitude, and reflects an interest in giving, whether that which is given is money, other financial assets, time, energy, or support. A spirit of generosity in a family brings with it a sense of abundance, counteracting perceptions of scarcity and thus preventing competition for resources. When a spirit of generosity pervades a family, people feel loved. They are more likely to be compassionate and to focus on what's best for *everyone*, including future generations. In fact, I often try to help wealth creators and family members to understand the role that generosity and gratitude can and do play in their estate plans. For example, I had a conversation with a wealth creator who insisted that he worked hard at estate planning primarily to enable better tax planning. When I pushed him for what underlay his

[13] Martin Seligman, *Learned Optimism* (Vintage, New York, 2006).

extensive efforts, he admitted it was his love for his children and grand-children that motivated him. He was mistaking genuine generosity for a need only to outmaneuver tax agencies through planning!

- *Mindfulness*: Mindfulness, is about living in the present, without judg-ment or second-guessing—being highly aware of what you're doing and why you're doing it. It applies to everything from diet (as opposed to mind*less* eating) to money (understanding where and why you spend) to relationships (understanding what you want from social ties and what you get—or don't get—from them).[14] In the context of wealth continuity planning, an understanding of mindfulness helps people to feel a greater sense of gratitude and leads to more enjoyable personal relationships.

- *Mastery/self-efficacy*: Finally, mastery and self-efficacy are personal quali-ties that contribute to feeling capable in multiple domains. Not surpris-ingly, that feeling of capability has been linked to overall satisfaction with life.[15] When we feel competent, it lends us a strong sense of confi-dence, even in areas that might be unfamiliar. For example, in my obser-vation, family members who feel effective in several domains—such as work, governance, relationships—are more likely to be engaged and to contribute more effectively to continuity plans and structures than those who lack that sense of self-efficacy.

What Is Your Family's Level of Commitment to Personal Development?

The following questions, based on this chapter's contents, can help you assess the level of your family's Commitment to Personal Development, or that of one you advise.

- Is your family situation marked by the presence of only a small number of members with strong financial and legal literacy?

---

[14] To learn more about mindfulness, see "Mindfulness Essential Reads," *Psychology Today*, https://www.psychologytoday.com/topics/mindfulness/essentials (accessed July 30, 2015).

[15] See for example Evangelos Karademas, "Self-efficacy, Social Support, and Well-being," *Personality and Individual Differences*, Volume 40, Issue 6, April 2006, Pages 1281–1290.

- Do members of your family struggle in vain to understand continuity structures, including trust documents and other such materials?
- Is there no or minimal collective interest in uncovering and encouraging individual members' needs, interests, and aspirations?
- Is there an over-emphasis on developing specific business-related or professional skills, rather than a wider range of capabilities and interests that members may have?
- Is there zero or limited effort to encourage financial and legal literacy (such as through books or formal and informal programs) in rising generation members from an early age?
- Do family members seem reluctant or afraid to ask questions related to continuity structures and other complex elements of the business or family?
- Is there a lack of self-awareness and empathy for other members at the individual level?
- Is the family marked by overconsumption or other elements that suggest an inability to delay gratification at individual or collective levels?
- Is there a lack of effort to help members develop emotional intelligence—or minimal response to problems related to emotional intelligence (such as frequent conflicts or other disruptive behavior)?
- Does the physical or mental health status of one or more family members cause disruption of family interaction and harmony?
- Is there a lack of emphasis on individuals' health and happiness, such as formal or informal programs to help family members reach higher levels of physical health, mindfulness, and self-efficacy?

Any "yes" answers to the questions above point out issues related to Commitment to Personal Development within your family. The presence of many "yes" answers indicates a significant problem related to such commitment, and warrants a much closer look at what your family can do to build this critical element of the Foundation for Family Wealth Continuity, using the ideas in this chapter and others.

Where Do You Stand?

In Fig. 5.3, place an X at the point along the column representing "Commitment to Personal Development" to indicate where you think your family stands with regard to strength on this building block. A score of "0"

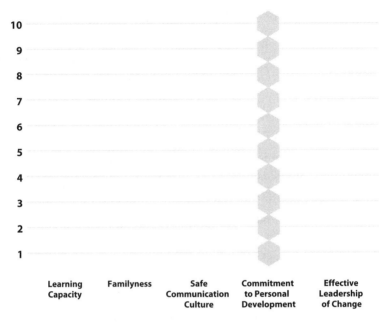

Fig. 5.3 Commitment to Personal Development: Your Rating

represents a very low Commitment to Personal Development overall, while 10 represents a very high level of commitment. Your ratings on all building blocks (including those discussed in other chapters) will give you a sense of how strong your overall Foundation for Family Wealth Continuity is.

What If a Family Commitment to Personal Development Is Unlikely?

As I noted above, ultimately a Commitment to Personal Development is *personal*. For various reasons, then, families may not subscribe to the point of view that *family* commitment to such development is important:

- It may be a "pull yourself up by the bootstraps" family culture
- There may be a misunderstanding or lack of understanding as to the connection between personal development and family wealth continuity
- The family may lack one or more of the building blocks already discussed (Learning Capacity, Familyness, Safe Communication Culture) and as such may compromise a personal development program.

No matter the reason, in all of these cases it once again comes down to the *personal* in personal development: Development is ultimately the responsibility of an individual. While I believe it is fundamental to long term wealth continuity, it is also fundamental to a person's capacity to live well in the present and under present circumstances. If a family Commitment to Personal Development is unlikely to evolve, then my best advice is for each willing individual or each willing group within the family—be it a branch or set of siblings or another faction—to pursue opportunities in this realm and to the extent possible to share the value and positive results with other family members either formally (via family meetings) or through informal personal conversations.

Points to Remember

The following are the key points to keep in mind from this chapter on Commitment to Personal Development:

- Commitment to Personal Development within a family reflects an interest in promoting the growth of individual members with regard to three key areas: financial and legal literacy, emotional intelligence, and the "two H's," or health and happiness.
- Families often under-estimate the importance of personal development, leaving only a small minority of members with the capabilities to engage in the process of continuity planning or over-emphasizing the importance of growth only in the professional domain. These situations virtually ensure that the planning will fail to engage a broad set of members, leaving them out of important decision-making processes.
- A healthy Commitment to Personal Development balances individual and collective needs over the long term without imposing a specific course of development on members.
- *Financial and legal literacy* can be developed from an early age through a conscious effort to educate and support family members through formal and informal programs (such as bringing in financial/legal experts to family meetings). Promoting a "no-stupid-questions" culture enables family members to ask about unfamiliar areas—including those related to continuity planning—and seek knowledge in these.
- *Emotional intelligence* includes the elements of self-awareness, empathy, delay of gratification, and general social skill. Empathy is a particularly important element relating to continuity planning, and it can be improved even by simple practices such as asking fellow family members

about their thoughts and feelings. Emotional intelligence in general may be enhanced by asking for feedback and practicing more effective social responses.

- *Health and happiness* are important to continuity planning because chronic issues in these areas for even one family member can disrupt family interactions and harmony. Families can promote individual members' health/happiness through both internal and external opportunities aimed at enhancing physical fitness, optimism, self-efficacy, and other facets.

- When a family's collective Commitment to Personal Development is unlikely to improve, individuals and groups within the family can take up the charge of promoting development on successively more inclusive levels.

CHAPTER 6

Effective Leadership of Change

"Are you sure you want this job?" I asked Hans in our first meeting. There seemed to be every reason the young man, the third-generation successor to his father as CEO of the family's $500 million business, would answer my question with a resounding "yes:" He was smart, well-educated, and energetic, with an infectious personality and a terrific business mind. From the firm's point of view, as Hans' father neared retirement, Hans was the right person to become the next CEO, having successfully managed a large, high-profile division of the company in a VP role and earned the respect of senior non-family managers.

So I was somewhat surprised when Hans said, "I'm not sure I'm ready." But the more we discussed his feelings and the family's situation, the more I understood his position. Over time he had found himself engaged in recurrent, frustrating interactions with his two uncles, both of whom were concerned he would treat their families less fairly than his father had. They inundated him with questions about multiple issues: "What will change regarding the family employment policy?" "How will your relationships with your cousins affect their opportunities with the business?" And many others. Hans had tried to appease both of his father's brothers, listening to their concerns and providing reassurance. But neither seemed satisfied. One uncle had pushed so hard that Hans had blown up at him in a recent family meeting.

In short, while Hans felt confident about his ability to handle future business issues as CEO, he was frustrated by the complex *non-business* issues related to leadership succession, as exemplified by his challenges dealing with his uncles. The family's dynamic represented major problems with effective leadership of change, and that was undermining any attempt at developing a feasible succession and a broader continuity plan.

Hans' family's situation illustrates the final building block in the Foundation for Family Wealth Continuity: Effective Leadership of Change. As I have emphasized throughout this book, continuity planning is about managing change and even transforming it from threat to opportunity over the long term, ensuring extensive family participation and commitment to the enterprise. That holds true whether we are talking about an estate plan, a family business succession plan, or a plan for a family office; all of these require overt and covert change on the part of family generations, branches, and members. And managing that change requires strong leadership.

What Is Effective Leadership of Change?

Effective development and implementation of a wealth continuity structure requires alignment among several "moving" parts: Family members' interests and skills, the collective vision of the business's and family's future, and the structures that have been created or proposed to make the vision a reality. In an ideal case, family leadership—including representatives and inputs from several generations—aligns all of these elements together into a coherent, unified whole. Thus Effective Leadership of Change in your family or one you advise is a key building block in the Foundation for Family Wealth Continuity as illustrated in Fig. 6.1.

The idea that leaders must handle change well or even seek it out should not come as a surprise to anyone. A recent *Forbes* article, for example, is titled, "How the Best Leaders Embrace Change."[1] But in family business, change, especially around continuity planning, can be seen as a challenge, a threat, or even something to be avoided at all costs. That's why I've devoted an entire chapter to effective leading of change.

Before we consider the dimensions of effective leadership, let's think about all the facets of *change* that must be navigated when it comes to continuity planning:

---

[1] Dorie Clark, "How the Best Leaders Embrace Change," *Forbes*, November 5, 2013, http://www.forbes.com/sites/dorieclark/2013/11/05/how-the-best-leaders-embrace-change/ (accessed October 6, 2015).

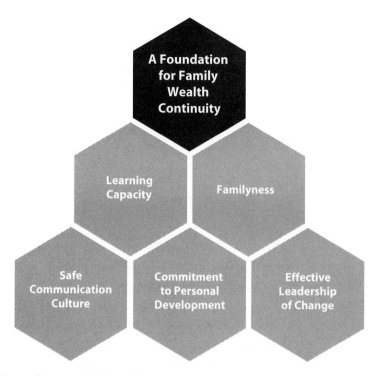

Fig. 6.1 Effective Leadership of Change

- *Who controls the assets*: Control of assets is typically at the core of any continuity plan. In a business succession plan, the change may be from a senior family member to a rising-generation member. In an estate plan, the transition may be from Mom and Dad controlling the assets to placing the assets under a trustee's control. In a family office, control over investment decisions might shift from a single family member or small number of members to more shared, collective decision-making.
- *Inheritance decisions*: Inheritance decisions naturally require adjustments or changes. An estate plan, for example, might prescribe generation-skipping transfers that could be perceived as the grandparents' having an impact upon, or even replacing, parental decisions about their children's' inheritance.
- *Practice of philanthropy*: Philanthropy can be a deceptively simple domain within wealth continuity planning. A family foundation might encourage family members to work together to decide on gifts and their recipients, but ultimate control over those decisions may reside with the

founder/wealth creator. Similarly, rising-generation members may be expected to participate in philanthropic activity, but philanthropic beneficiaries might be restricted to the geographic region where the wealth was originally created, where most family members no longer reside.

- *Marital pre-conditions*: Accepting an inheritance or participating in family office services may require changes such as asking family members to agree to a prenuptial agreement that stipulates the disposition of assets—an agreement crafted by a wealth creator and his/her attorneys, rather than by the parties actually marrying.
- *Meeting requirements*: Family members are often required to travel to attend family, shareholder, or trustee meetings. The implementation of a family governance system could mean more—and more frequent—family meetings that require travel and time away from studies, work, or home, which represents another significant change.
- *Values*: Expectations regarding values represent yet another, often challenging form of change. For example, a family constitution may articulate values that are at odds with the personal values of individual family members who may nevertheless be asked to subscribe to the constitution in order to participate in governance, business-related activities, or even inheritance.
- *Communication*: Changes extend to communication-related do's and don'ts. With the advent of a family council, for instance, family members may learn that individuals are discouraged from speaking to managers or board members individually, though they may have done so in the past.

Even when some or all of the building blocks discussed in previous chapters are in place—Learning Capacity, Familyness, Safe Communication Culture, and Commitment to Personal Development, specifically—the changes described above and the many others that are prescribed for a family as wealth continuity structures evolve are best introduced and stewarded by effective leaders who have some basic understanding and appreciation of the family dynamics that accompany change, and how to manage these dynamics. After all, as described above, most continuity plans prescribe not only the disposition of assets, but the management of behavior as well, including attending family council meetings, taking part in educational activities related to rising-generation ownership roles, adhering to values and practices the family has agreed to, and many others.

Thus the implementation process must account for real human constraints: behavior change, particularly on a family-wide scale is very challenging. I don't know about you, but something even as "simple" as trying to get my adult children together for a one-week vacation is always much more difficult than I expect it to be! In that context, leading the implementation of long-term wealth continuity structures that require various degrees of behavior change can be overwhelmingly complex and challenging. Not impossible, but difficult. And that difficulty often falls on the shoulders of a family member or non-family advisor entrusted with the task of implementing the changes.

We have touched on this issue of leadership in various ways in previous chapters, by pointing out the multifaceted factors any planning-focused leader will face. But in this chapter we address the topic head on, with perspectives and practices for leading change effectively.

The Challenges of Change: A Systems View

I suggested in my introduction to this book that families are systems. A system may be described in terms of two primary components: "content" and "process." The *content* of a system refers to items and events that are readily observable by outsiders looking into the system. In the system we know as an ocean, for example, the content would include water, sand, marine life, and easily observable patterns among these, such as schools of fish swimming in the water, among others. Thus the content may change from time to time and from place to place—different oceans have different contents, depending on time and place. The *process* of a system, in contrast, is the "how" of the system: how the contents are related and work together—or don't—as part of the system, often in subtle ways that might be more difficult to observe. In the ocean, that would include the interrelationships between the environment and the range of creatures that inhabit it—both short—and long-term—along with the dynamics of the sea creatures, within and among different groups.

In the case of a family, the main content comprises the people and the environment in which they reside, along with their typical interactions. The patterns underlying their repetitive sequences of individual or collective behavior constitute their process, or family dynamics. Consider how these concepts play into the following family business example.

Leonard was the third-generation president of his family's billion-dollar manufacturing company. The company had been started by Leonard's grandfather, and Leonard, now in his late 40s, had assumed the presidency from his father two years ago. Leonard's father, now in his mid-70s and still the chairman of the firm's board, had transferred 95% of the company stock to Leonard and his two younger brothers, but retained 100% of voting control with his wife (the mother of Leonard and his siblings). Leonard was quite comfortable as the business's president, and saw himself as a future leader of the family, as did his brothers. In that capacity, he made repeated efforts on his own and his brothers' behalf to engage his parents in a meaningful estate planning process—especially around the future of the voting shares, and the goal of transferring assets out of his parents' taxable estate. But each time Leonard tried to bring up the topic, whether by appealing to logic, invoking the advice of attorneys, or describing planning examples set by other business families, his efforts were rebuffed by his father with remarks from one or more of the categories below:

- *Practical*: "We're too busy running the company to spend time on something like that!"
- *Reassuring*: "Don't worry. It will be taken care of."
- *Questioning*: "Why are you so concerned about our estate?"

Not surprisingly, each time this happened, Leonard and his brothers felt increasingly frustrated, helpless, and angry. Their feelings had the natural but unintended effect of escalating into shouting matches that shut down all communication between the siblings and their parents, sometimes for weeks at a time. Once everyone had cooled down, usually on their mother's urging, the family would return to more civil interactions, and Leonard would strive to act as a good family leader. But the topic of estate and wealth transfer planning eventually arose again, always ending poorly. And so the cycle continued.

In this unfortunately realistic and common example, the content had to do with the family members and their interactions related to estate planning and wealth transfer; the process might be described as an effort to engage in logical discourse, followed by reluctance and denial, followed by redoubled efforts, followed by anger, escalation, and a communication shutdown.

So, from a systems point of view, what seems to be straightforward *content* (family members engaging in wealth continuity planning) is often much more complex due to *challenging process* (family dynamics). Effective leadership will help family members understand and address the disruptive role of process/dynamics in planning-related change, smoothing the way for effective development and implementation.

Understanding Homeostasis

In Chap. 3, I discussed how family systems tend to thrive on stability. More specifically, an *unstable* family system, in which members are unpredictable and emotions generally run high, faces numerous risks: emotional cut-offs, estrangement, frequent arguments, and inability to spend comfortable time together or to collaborate. Clearly, for families who wish to preserve shared interests related to both family and business, this is unacceptable. So healthy families tend to engage in behavior patterns—family dynamics—that will help them preserve stability.

In biological systems, this tendency is known as homeostasis. For example, a human biological mechanism of homeostasis is perspiration, which uses evaporation to help maintain a stable body temperature. Families tend toward homeostasis as well—when communication in Leonard's family (see earlier example) shuts down for a period of time, the pause allows the family system to "reset" to "restabilize" and to return to some degree of normal functioning, a sort of equilibrium, if you will. In Leonard's family, then, the cooling off period acted much like perspiration does in the human body, allowing a return to a more stable state (though a short-lived one in that family's case).

Effective family leaders of change need to understand the difference between healthy and unhealthy disruptions of homeostasis. Rancorous, repeated family interactions such as bitter arguments and name-calling, for example, are obviously unhealthy disruptions and should be prevented or dealt with actively to avoid recurrence. Other "disruptions" might be associated with healthier change, such as Leonard's justified attempts to engage the family in estate planning. When such disruption is met with resistance and reluctance, it might preserve short-term homeostasis but lead to longer-term issues and conflicts that will *prevent* homeostasis. Again, effective leaders take steps to foster healthy dialogue around healthy change, preserving longer-term equilibrium.

The trick, then, is to see homeostasis not as a static state—in part because family dynamics change so much from day to day—but a long-term environment of equilibrium in which family members feel involved, heard, and understood, especially when it comes to continuity planning. They see (and use) family dynamics as an *opportunity* for effective intervention, rather than viewing them as an insurmountable threat to the family's well-being and future.

What Lies Beneath

The concept of homeostasis leads to discussion of another concept that leaders of family change should be aware of: How *underlying factors* can drive behavior in the family system that may not seem wholly rational from an outsider's perspective. Even the most successful families seem irrational at times. There's a good reason for this: Many of the events, interactions, and decisions that occur in families emerge from, are reactions to, or are influenced by emotions, relationships, and personal history—underlying factors—that are not outwardly apparent. Therefore, what may appear irrational to an outsider may in fact be a very reasonable reaction to unseen or unknown family events, histories, or feelings. Families have an internal logic which, when fully understood, provides a key that transforms the irrational to rational, or at least helps it make more sense.

For example, in Leonard's family, the reluctance to engage in any estate planning for owners of a billion-dollar company might seem like a terribly irrational act on the surface. However, if you knew that Leonard's father and mother were in constant disagreement as to whether the company's voting shares should be passed on to Leonard alone, equally to the three siblings, or in some kind of proportion to their involvement in the business (Leonard was much more involved than his siblings), then the reluctance to engage in estate planning does not seem so irrational!

The point here is that family leaders of change need to be willing and able to look beyond the ostensibly logical and understand that some of the challenges to introducing change in the family may be a result of factors that are not immediately apparent. This has implications for understanding the family's behavior as well as for a leader's efforts to manage family change. If the introduction of multi-dimensional change via a continuity plan is met with resistance and reluctance, even after repeated appeals to logic, then "more of the same" (that is, more appeals to logic, whether in the form of reasoned arguments, invocation of "best practices," or pointing out the experiences of others) is unlikely to result in a different outcome. The effective leader of family change who encounters such resistance is well-advised to consider other, previously unrecognized dynamics that may be causing an impasse.

Let's think about what some of these underlying dynamics might be:

- *Fear of the unknown.* Why are children—and many adults, for that matter—afraid of diving off a high-board into a swimming pool? Because they have never experienced that exact sensation before and worry that it might be difficult for them. Almost nobody, maybe with the exception of the true daredevils among us, wants to jump into the deep end, whether literal or figurative, without having a good idea of what they will experience. For example, I worked with one family on development of a very important transition plan: Structuring their board such that board members were there not there so much to represent branches but to contribute to business governance and to enhance the entire family's chances for a successful transition between generations. Many family members opposed the idea. "We have always represented our branch" one family board member said to me. "How do we know that your recommendation won't make things worse for us?" She continued. It was a reasonable question, even though the family had experienced a constant battle over equal representation for the branches. In such situations, the saying "Better the devil you know than the one you don't" is particularly apt, as families will often take a difficult but familiar situation over an unfamiliar but potentially better one. Managing fear of the unknown will require some appeal to logic, but ultimately will depend on the trust that family members have in their leader(s) to make changes that will ultimately benefit them all. In this example, the family, with my help, eventually trusted their leaders and made the change to less branch focus on the board, resulting quickly in better family unity and progress toward the continuity plan.

- *Mortality.* Continuity planning, and the estate-planning dimension in particular, often raise issues related to endings: end of a generation, end of a family "era," end of an individual. Mortality is a difficult issue for anyone: seniors, family members, advisors, and other stakeholders. That's why such discussions are frequently avoided. One way to approach this is the way you would eat an elephant: one bite at a time! In behavioral psychology this is called "successive approximations," or the development of a complex behavior or response by breaking it down into small steps and achieving each one. For example, a person who's afraid of spiders might be asked to imagine a spider, then to look at pictures of spiders, then to be across the room from a small spider, then to move closer to it, and so on, until they can comfortably be near a spider (if that's their goal!). The idea is to aim for change one step at a time, and the same principle can be applied to difficult conversations around mortality. In that case, it's best not to push the conversation to a point of anger, but repeatedly raising the issue and trying to manage it in small parts can be helpful. For example, if the delicate issue at hand is estate planning, then a first step could be discussing where the related financial documents are, or designating family members as signatories on bank accounts. One step, then another, then another.

- *Permanence.* Another underlying factor may be the permanence of many continuity plans. In particular, certain estate-planning vehicles and the loss of control that accompanies them are irrevocable. For example, an irrevocable trust for the benefit of one's grandchildren would transfer assets out of a wealth creator's estate to reduce his or her estate taxes. However, thereafter the trust cannot be modified or terminated without the permission of the beneficiaries. Thus, for all intents and purposes the wealth creator permanently relinquishes all of his or her rights to the assets in the trust. So there may need to be understanding and acceptance that giving up some control and acceding to permanent changes are a reasonable price to pay for greater security for current and future generations of the family.

Apathy and Inertia

While a search for the underlying factors that influence change might reveal complex emotions and motivations, sometimes change is difficult simply due to apathy or inertia—it's often easier to do nothing than to do something! Newton's First Law of Motion states that objects at rest tend to stay at rest, and that it takes the application of external force to set a resting object in motion or to change its course if already in motion. I like to think that families, like physical objects, are subject to the laws of nature. In this case, families may be challenged by the prospect of change that is brought about by continuity planning simply because change requires the application of energy. Many families are simply so engaged in their day-to-day activities, that investing the energy in change is just not possible.

So the effective leader of change in a family will need to consider how to overcome the influence of inertia that may impede effective implementation of continuity plans. Some strategies to consider in this respect include:

- Clarifying family priorities so that implementation of a continuity plan is viewed as a priority, at least in the short- term.

- Delegating tasks and distributing responsibilities so that the energy required for good implementation is shared and not the responsibility of only one or two parties.
- Bringing in outside advisors who may add perspective and energy to the process.

Psychological Reactance

Some resistance to change takes a much more *active* form than inertia. One particularly powerful factor at play in resistance to changes associated with continuity planning—whether overt or covert—can be psychological reactance. Put simply, psychological reactance occurs when a person sees his or her choices as limited by an external factor, and reacts by adopting a contrarian point of view, attitude, or behavior.[2] As you could imagine, reactance occurred in Leonard's family when he and his siblings redoubled efforts to convince their parents to engage in estate and wealth-transfer planning. The elder generation's resistance had less to do with logic (continuity planning is a perfectly logical activity), and more to do with the parents feeling that their children were constraining their choices related to the planning—specifically, when to have focused discussions about it. The more their children pushed, the greater their reactance and associated resistance.

We can think of the sources of reactance as representing several categories:

- *The actions of others*: When someone imposes something overtly on someone else, as was the case in Leonard's family, the second party is likely to demonstrate reactance.
- *The expectations of others*: Reactance can also result from the expectations of others, rather than their overt actions. A common example in family business is when the founding or senior generation expects the rising generation to join the business, even if this is never communicated directly. Not surprisingly, the mere presence of that expectation can and often does induce the rising generation to have mixed feelings about joining the business and may cause some family members to avoid the business entirely.

[2] For more on the phenomenon of and evidence for psychological reactance, see Sharon Brehm and Jack Brehm, *Psychological Reactance: A Theory of Freedom and Control* (Academic Press, New York, 1981).

- *Structures in place*: Continuity structures, rather than people, can also cause reactance. For example, a trust with strict limits on access to funds might make the beneficiaries fight for greater access, even if they don't necessarily have a specific need in mind.

In my experience, when people believe they do not have a choice or that others are limiting their choices, they tend to do two things: they push back *and* they spend much of their time thinking about how to remove whatever constraints they perceive. In the Familyness chapter, we discussed a variant of reactance as "imposed mutuality," or when family members feel compelled to be together by other parties' (in this case, other family members, usually the senior generation) decisions or expectations that may not reflect the choice of all individuals involved; we discussed this as an instance of excessive Familyness, and it could result in an unwillingness or uneasiness on the part of members to spend time together. But reactance has much broader additional implications for wealth continuity planning. I discuss one such issue in the "Planning in a Vacuum" box below.

Planning in a Vacuum

It is not uncommon for wealth continuity plans to be made without taking into consideration those for whom the plans are crafted. I call this "Planning in a Vacuum." As an illustration, in one family a very large foundation was funded with over $100 million. The founder's goals were to have his children and adult grandchildren serve on the foundation's board. So he was hurt and frustrated when all three of his children eventually resigned from the board and none of his grandchildren were interested in the first place. Though his feelings may have seemed justified on the surface, in reality the founder had created a foundation that reflected only *his* philanthropic goals and had made clear that no other causes would be funded. So this was a case of a wealth continuity structure that was properly executed but poorly realized, with reactance as a clear factor. The founder in the example had "planned in a vacuum," rather than taking the needs or interests of rising generations in mind. Doing so might have prevented the reactance-fueled dismissal of the founder's wishes by the younger generations.

Reactance can even lead to behaviors that seem to go against one's own interests. In the family behind a large retail hardware business in the southern

US, for example, a family-member trustee and a trusted financial advisor made every decision regarding the investment of significant assets held in trust for three siblings. For close to 20 years the investment decisions made were smart, timely, and successful in building the family's wealth. The siblings, however, had been excluded from investment meetings for many years, at first because of their age and then ostensibly because they "had no investment experience." As they entered adulthood they were literally told to "be quiet and be happy with your distributions." Little effort was made to teach them anything about investing. On their own, the siblings—quietly—began to gather knowledge about their legal rights, and when they learned that they could remove the trustee and her advisor, they did so immediately. When the trustee learned that the beneficiaries were moving to have her removed, she was aghast, claiming that her investment performance was "beyond reproach." But it was never the investment performance that was in question; it was the siblings' lack of choice in the matter, which led, perhaps understandably, to reactance and consequent action that may have posed some risk to their financial future. However, as this example illustrates, choice and the freedom it reflects are sometimes perceived as more valuable than an incremental shift in investment performance.

It may not be all that surprising, then, that it has been estimated that 98 % of inheritors replace the investment advisors in place when they come into their inheritance.[3] The incumbent advisors may be perfectly capable, but the heirs often want some choice or say in the matter, and they tend to exercise it swiftly once available. In my view, family members who feel they have no input in fundamental decisions that affect them will at best lack commitment to a wealth continuity structure; at worst they will work hard to unwind any plans that have been made, even those which may appear to be in their collective best interest.

Given the challenges posed by reactance, inertia, and other underlying factors, how should effective leaders of family change proceed? One of the most important priorities is the creation of a culture of informed choice, as discussed next.

---

[3] As cited by Michael Sisk, "How to Keep the Kids," *Barrons*, June 4, 2011, http://www.barrons.com/articles/SB50001424053111904210704576357873121823708 (accessed October 8, 2015).

A Culture of Informed Choice

Choice is critical to furthering family engagement in the planning process. Effective leaders of change understand this. But choice alone is not sufficient; *informed* choice is critical. Family members should be prepared to make well-educated choices to engage most effectively. An example illustrates this concept well.

In a family that owned a large US manufacturing business, Catherine, the youngest sister, had lived in Europe for many years after marrying an Italian native. From young adulthood, she'd had frequent, sustained conflict with her father, and returned to visit the family only rarely, with minimal contact between trips. Upon her father's death, Catherine inherited one quarter of the company's shares, but none of the voting stock—because her father did not trust her to act in the business's best interests. Her three siblings had each inherited a quarter of the company stock as well, and one third of the voting stock. All three had worked in the company their entire careers, and had learned to collaborate well, voting as a block on every major business decision.

During the early period after their father's passing, Catherine moved back to the US, but her siblings continued to treat her as an outsider, as intended by their father. She was refused a seat on the board and her comments at shareholder meetings were routinely dismissed or ignored. Naturally, this did not sit well with Catherine, and she stirred up trouble at every meeting, challenging her siblings and even causing them to turn against one another on occasion, something that had never happened before.

While the two middle siblings expressed frustration and suggested finding ways to bar Catherine from the meetings, her oldest brother, the company's CEO, took a different approach: He explained to his siblings how he understood and empathized with Catherine about being excluded from the voting stock, and that her behavior was clearly a reaction to what she perceived as an insult. He also understood that her behavior could—in some ways already had—undermine family cohesiveness and threaten the overall success of the ownership succession plan.

So he proposed a plan to enable Catherine to feel more included and, potentially, to have more input. Specifically, he arranged for sibling meetings to occur before every board meeting, primarily as an opportunity for Catherine to ask questions and share her opinions; he had Catherine meet regularly with a non-family board member to develop more accurate knowledge of the company; he coached Catherine on how to present her comments more palatably; and he advised his siblings to make more space for Catherine's ideas. Through her brother's thoughtful, effective leadership, Catherine came to feel more a part of the family and its decision-making and was able to provide valuable input, even though she remained a non-voting shareholder.

Family leaders can take away several points from that example, as related to practical steps for creating a culture of informed choice:

1. *Recognize that choice is an inherent, desirable value for family members.* As such, constraints on choice will typically have a negative impact on the introduction of new plans and processes. Enabling people to have choice, and providing space in which to express diverse, sometimes divergent opinions (or "voice") will greatly reduce the challenge of change.

2. *Understand that choice and the expression of voice should not result in a "free for all."* This is the "informed" part of the concept. Choice should not be offered in a vacuum, but with proper educational opportunities, such that people understand basic financial and legal concepts (see the Commitment to Self-Development chapter for more on this) and details of any planning matters at hand. Ensuring informed choice and voice will curtail dramatically the proportion of superfluous, irrelevant, or even damaging inputs to the planning process, promoting a better outcome.

3. *Find opportunities to improve voice.* Along with opportunities to create an environment of choice, there are likely ways of helping people improve how they *express* their choices, as noted in the example used above. Approaches from simple, respectful feedback to the hiring of communication consultants and coaches may be used to ensure any communication around continuity planning is effective and well-received.

Used effectively, these steps can create an environment and culture of informed choice that engages family members and brings out their best, most thoughtful inputs. Family leaders may consider making the exercise of choice contingent on certain engagement-related criteria. That could be accomplished, for example, by requiring courses in financial and legal literacy before being able to offer investment input. Or it could mean conducting multiple site visits to the non-profits funded by the family's foundation before joining the foundation's board. Similarly, several business programs including those at the Kellogg School of Management (at Northwestern University), Harvard, UCLA, and Loyola University in Chicago offer family business governance and leadership workshops.[4] Some families make contributions to planning and governance contingent on attendance at such programs. In this way, an individual member's right to exercise choice may be tied to his or her commitment to and engagement with an overall continuity plan and the family more broadly. The "When Choice Becomes Imposition" box below describes another important dimension of the planning process for leaders to keep in mind.

When Choice Becomes Imposition

Even among families who seek to sustain a culture of informed choice, over time, choice can become imposition. This is a natural result of change across generations. For example, the leading generation of a family may develop a charter reflecting their values and priorities for a family office. That choice may represent that generation's interests very well, having been the product of good, inclusive collaboration. But as their children and grandchildren become engaged with the family office, what began as a choice for one generation of leaders may then become an imposition on the rising leaders of the next generation. So informed choice in one generation may become imposition in the next, in a continuing cycle. While this cycle may seem like a dilemma for some families, it can be a *healthy* dilemma: If the structures currently in place are respected and valued, viewed as dynamic, living, flexible and subject to change, then a family with a good foundation in place will find that wealth continuity structures can evolve over time, preserving what is valued from the past while introducing change in the present.

The value of choice in continuity planning is being recognized as US laws related to estate planning have changed over time. These changes have provided for the creation of wealth continuity structures—specifically, financial trusts—that promote and permit choice for certain beneficiaries. A detailed discussion of specific structures is beyond the scope of this book but, briefly,

---

[4] For more on the Kellogg School's family business programs, for example, see http://www.kellogg.northwestern.edu/execed/programs/fambiz.aspx.

state laws that provide for "multi-participant trusts" allow a separation of administrative, custodial, and investment trustee functions. Under these provisions, beneficiaries can choose to separate various trustee functions and assign investment oversight, for example, to an entity of their choosing. Thus new laws enable more choice and flexibility with regard to the implementation of planning structures than was available to families in the past, with benefits accruing to families aligned with the qualities in the discussion above.

The Practices of an Effective Family Change Agent

In this section I discuss specific concepts, qualities, and practices embraced by effective family leaders to navigate the challenges of change. While these practices apply to leaders of change who strive to implement wealth continuity structures, the practices may be applied more generally by family leaders of change who seek to understand and manage the family dynamics that may affect their leadership.

- *Understand that families are about dreams and relationships.* The smart leader understands that he or she is not just implementing a structure such as a business succession plan or family foundation, but is helping to manage the individual and collective dreams and relationships of the family, and how these two important elements interact. Paying attention to these elements—as much as, or more than the structures themselves—helps to ensure that family members accept and are engaged with the continuity plans. For example, an ownership succession plan that includes family members who have grown up with a business but haven't worked in it themselves, may have the potential to fulfill certain dreams of family leading to good engagement and implementation; a plan that does not include those family members, while perfectly adequate technically, may violate certain dreams, and implementation may suffer as a result.
- *Emphasize stewardship.* "In any continuity plan, consider first what you want to preserve, not what you want to change," says my colleague and family business expert John L. Ward.[5] Thus effective leaders bear in mind the "continuity" component of continuity planning, by placing value on stewardship. That means leading with respect for what has

[5] John L. Ward, personal communication, October 2014.

come before and seeking to preserve that, while implementing change. In this context, stewardship refers not only to the financial assets that a family values, but also to the structures that have been in place, and to the relationships that exist among family members.

- *Articulate a clear vision.* Family leaders need a clear sense of what change is leading to: What is the overall purpose of a wealth continuity structure? How will family benefit? What costs may be involved? Effective leaders are able to articulate a clear sense of their vision in a narrative or a story that connects meaningfully and on an emotional level with those for whom plans are being made. A rising leader of the next generation who is designated as the next CEO of the family office is unlikely to have an enthusiastic following among family if her narrative is simply "No one else can do the job," even if she is the perfect family member for the job. By contrast, a narrative that describes her vision for how others will be engaged, the benefits that will accrue, and the value of carrying on, is likely to bring far more success.

- *Ally with the system.* Strong leaders earn trust not just through competence, vision, and honesty, but also by allying themselves with the system they are trying to change. That is reflected in a full range of behaviors: Asking questions to understand what motivates people and what makes them nervous; encouraging and modeling a culture of listening within the family; mirroring the language and behavior of others to show respect and understanding for them; showing empathy by validating the difficulties associated with change and the frustration members may feel about these. Such approaches make the leader a genuine ally of the system rather than someone imposing unpopular ideas on it.

- *Provide honest feedback.* Effective leadership includes the ability to observe the system and provide honest and incisive feedback, as described in the chapter on learning Capacity. One way for leaders to accomplish this is by taking a position of "in it, not of it": that is, being part of the family system while being able to take a step back and assume a more objective, detached viewpoint. This capacity requires a considerable degree of self-awareness—the ability to recognize the role you are playing in the system—and the capacity to comment on the system candidly without making family members defensive. For example, a rising leader was struggling with the detachment of his cousins as ownership was being transferred to that generation. He was able to look objectively at this situation, share his disappointment with his cousins, while also sharing that he could have been doing a better job including them in various important decisions. I've seen some effective leaders use what I call the "Columbo approach," named after the famous TV-show detective played by Peter Falk in the 1970s. Columbo outsmarted criminals by playing dumb and asking innocent-seeming questions to get them to confess. In the wealth continuity planning context, such a question might be something like, "I may be wrong about this but it seems to me that you all are having a hard time engaging in this meeting. What do you think?" By posing it as a question, and by taking a "one-down" position admitting that you might be wrong, the observation can be shared without raising defensiveness while simultaneously opening a dialogue. That strategic approach to honesty makes people more willing to hear feedback and become part of change rather than resisting it.

- *Clarify roles and expectations.* To lead effectively, a family member, particularly one of the rising generation, needs to be recognized and accepted in that role. No amount of hard work, coaxing, or appeals to loyalty or legacy will ensure the efficacy of one's leadership if that role is not clearly supported by the family at large. Resistance and reluctance to implementation are not necessarily signs that a structure is faulty; the parties leading implementation may not be recognized properly in that role. In one family, a senior family member designated his son as the member who should be leading implementation of a family council; he had a very hard time in that role until he asked his siblings and cousins for their support. The simple act of asking for support—not assuming it—made all the difference in this family's success.

- *Discover exceptions to negative perspectives.* "This family never communicates about real issues," a family member might say, or "We never listen to each other." Wise leaders validate such concerns while also asking about exceptions to the generalizations they represent. "Can you remember a time we talked about something meaningful?" they might ask. "Do you recall a time a family member listened to you, even if just once? What was different about that situation?" Finding such exceptions is important because it opens people to the idea that they may be overgeneralizing and builds on the positive rather than feeding the negative, contributing to a more inspiring, forward-looking narrative. Note how the leader *asks* about exceptions rather than actively disagreeing with the speaker by pointing out counter-examples, such that it's a process of mutual discovery that the family member is more likely to own.

- *Calm the system.* The best leaders inspire enthusiasm while having the capacity to calm things down as well. Behaviors in this realm can range from maintaining a calm presence when presenting plans or discussing change—as far as tone of voice, breathing, and body language—to assisting family members to manage their emotional reactions and take an objective perspective on pending changes.[6]

- *Reframe non-alignment.* Reframing interpretations is one method that is useful when calming the family system. As noted earlier, there are many good reasons why implementation is difficult in a family, including the dynamics of homeostasis, underlying factors, and apathy and inertia. So reluctance to change is natural and normal. Effective family leaders recognize this and give themselves and other family members "permission" to feel reluctant as change is implemented or to question vision and goals. In one family a discussion around leadership succession in the family office led to open dialogue about historical resentments in the family; shortly after this dialogue began, one of the cousins got up from the table and left the room, saying he was not ready to discuss these issues. Rather than impulsively reacting to this conversation stopper, the designated next-generation leader of the family office wisely stated, "These things take time to work through, and this is a good message to all of us to slow down our process." "Reframing," means providing an alternative interpretation of events. In this case, the alternative was to view the conversation-stopper as a good message to all rather than as a disruptive factor.

- *Communicate openly and often.* I can't emphasize enough the value of open and frequent communication around the implementation of wealth continuity structures. Every building block discussed thus far relies at least in part on good communication. The effective leader recognizes the value in good communication: Updating participants, keeping

---

[6] For more on the principles and practice that can be used to reduce anxiety, see Judith Beck, *Cognitive Behavior Therapy: Basics and Beyond* (Guilford Press, New York, 2011).

them informed and posing good questions are all activities that can help secure good engagement.

Who Should Lead?

In this final section, I raise the question of *who* should lead the changes that are to be brought about by continuity plans. Several points are worth noting.

Throughout this book I have provided guidance on methods to manage challenges, deficiencies, and perceived weaknesses in a family's Foundation for Family Wealth Continuity. I encourage readers to explore these methods, and it will be natural for a family leader of change to assume some or most of the responsibility for doing so. However, this book is not a training manual. There are circumstances—as I have emphasized at various points in the book—where family change is frankly so much of a challenge that it is most prudent not to undertake it at all, or at best, to rely on the close assistance of a trained facilitator.

For example, when a family's profile (which will be described in more detail in the next chapter) demonstrates weakness in all the prior building blocks—Learning Capacity, Familyness, Safe Communication Culture, and Commitment to Personal Development—the challenge of change will be substantial. In this circumstance an attempt to lead change might at best be frustrating; at worst, it might "inoculate" family against change in the future by creating an experience of failure. It will take full consideration of the issues outlined in the previous chapters, good judgment, and a little bit of wisdom for leaders to arrive at the right conclusion as to whether and when change should be targeted and by whom.

Remember, one key principle in my writing this book, is that sometimes, under some circumstances, for some families, efforts to keep family and assets together for generations is *not* a good idea. In these situations the best leaders will consider several options:

- Pursue specific training and educational opportunities that will advance your capacity for implementing change in a family. Conferences on family business and family wealth often include segments on various related topics: See below for further discussion of this topic.
- Consult with and retain a good facilitator, trained in family governance and family dynamics, to assist with a change effort.

- Consider how best to communicate the downside of change to a family: Why a wealth continuity structure may not be feasible in this family at this time, perhaps using the ratings and observations culled from reading previous chapters in this book. In this case, a leader's role may be less about implementing change and more about assisting the family to accept the reality that a goal of keeping assets and family together through a wealth continuity structure is unrealistic.

It is not unusual, of course, for a senior family member or wealth creator to assume a leadership role in implementing a wealth continuity structure: After all, it is probably his or her plan in the first place! However, members of a founding generation—and in particular, founders themselves—may have difficulty adjusting to many of the changes that have been promoted in previous chapters as important elements in the implementation of wealth continuity structures.[7] These elements prescribe transparency, inclusiveness, and focus on relationships and individual development, and usually mark a departure from the way things have been done in the past. Thus, I am recommending that founders and leaders of the rising generation take a good hard look at their own personal capacity for change, that they be realistic and honest, and if change is indeed the goal, then be clear that the person leading change should be ready and able to accept and support departures from the past.

How Effective Is Your Family's Leadership of Change?

The following questions, based on this chapter's contents, can help you assess the effectiveness of your family's leadership of change, or that of one you advise.

- Do your family leaders fail to differentiate between healthy and unhealthy disruptions or fail to take steps to address unhealthy interactions such as bitter arguments?
- Are key members of your family deeply resistant to change, whether the result of a fear of the unknown, reluctance to think about mortality,

---

[7] For more on the specific challenges family business founders and CEOs face in thinking about succession, continuity, and loss of control—along with advice for overcoming these—see Craig Aronoff and Otis Baskin, *Letting Go: Preparing Yourself to Relinquish Control of the Family Business* (Palgrave Macmillan, New York, 2010).

or unwillingness to engage in planning that might involve permanent change?

- Is there a general sense of inertia in your family, such that members are unlikely to enact change on important dimensions, even when it might benefit the family?
- Is there a pattern of significant reactance in your family, where members react to perceived imposition by pushing back, rather than having the parties involved engage in conversation about the issue?
- Does your family lack a culture of choice, where members feel comfortable expressing their interests or asking difficult questions about roles, responsibilities, and planning?
- Alternatively, does your family suffer from *too much* expression of choice, such that members offer uninformed, often clashing opinions on the best route forward in planning and other areas?
- Do leaders in your family fail to understand the importance of individual dreams and relationships when it comes to developing and implementing planning structures?
- Do leaders avoid or struggle to clarify key roles and expectations in the family—including their own and those of other members?
- Do leaders tend to add stress to the family system rather than calming it in times of uncertainty or adversity?
- Do leaders fail to communicate openly and often with the broader family about issues related to the business, planning, governance, or other areas?

Any "yes" answers to the questions above point out issues related to leadership of change within your family. The presence of many "yes" answers indicates a significant problem on this dimension, and warrants a much closer look at what your family can do to build this critical element of the Foundation for Family Wealth Continuity, using the ideas in this chapter and others.

Where Do You Stand?

In Fig. 6.2, place an X at the point along the column representing "Effective Leadership of Change" to indicate where you think your family stands with regard to strength on this building block. A score of "0" represents very low effectiveness on this dimension, while 10 represents the presence of high Effective Leadership of Change. Your ratings on all building blocks (including those discussed in other chapters) will give you a sense of the strength of your overall Foundation for Family Wealth Continuity.

What If Effective Leadership of Change Is Unlikely?

Some families may be less likely to foster Effective Leadership of Change among current members. This may be due to a lack of natural leaders among current generations, or to a lack of skill among current leaders. In such cases, effective implementation of wealth continuity structures will be an ongoing challenge, and following the advice presented so far in this chapter may be insufficient to resolve the issues.

Potential steps to take in this situation include:

- *Find new leaders*: In larger families, it may be possible that someone in the extended family is capable of leading effectively, including a family member who may not have been considered initially. This may be the

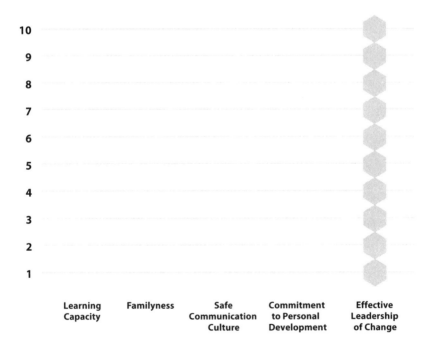

Fig. 6.2　Effective Leadership of Change: Your Rating

case because business leaders are frequently tasked to be family leaders as well, whereas family members who are *not* involved in an operating company may actually be a better choice because they embody more of the people skills necessary for implementing change. In other instances, it may be of value to delegate leadership to a non-family member, such as a capable board member or outside consultant. Finally, a co-leadership structure, one that includes a business leader and a family leader, may provide a good combination of the requisite skills for effective implementation.

- *Seek leadership training*: General leadership training is available through programs such as the Center for Creative Leadership.[8] Harvard, Kellogg, and other universities offer leadership training focused specifically on the challenges of family business, including continuity planning.[9] Beyond formal training, coaching and mentoring of potential leaders by board members, outside consultants, or others may also be of benefit

- *Accept the situation*: Finally, as noted above, if good leadership of change does not seem feasible in your family, consideration must be given to the possibility that implementation is simply not a good idea at this time.

Following these suggestions can hopefully help establish the right kind of leadership for the change that continuity planning inevitably introduces.

Points to Remember

The following are the key points to keep in mind from this chapter on Effective Leadership of Change:

- Effective family leaders align members' interest and skills with the collective vision of the family to create structures that make that vision a reality, while also managing the inevitable changes associated with continuity planning, from who controls the assets, to how the family's values are sustained and modified as implementation proceeds.

- It can be helpful to view change from a *systems perspective*, where family members and planning structures represent the "content" of the system

[8] For more on CCL programs, see http://www.ccl.org/Leadership/index.aspx (accessed October 22, 2015).

[9] For more on Kellogg's family leadership program, for example, see http://www.kellogg.northwestern.edu/execed/programs/famlead.aspx (accessed October 22, 2015).

and their dynamics represent the "process;" dynamics influence the family's ability to implement structures effectively, adding complexity to the challenge. A family system will move toward *homeostasis*.

- *Underlying factors* that complicate continuity planning and other processes, include fear of the unknown (the family's future), avoidance of discussions of mortality, and concern about instituting structures that imply permanent change.

- Other factors that pose challenges for leaders include *inertia* among members and *reactance*, or the tendency to push back actively against imposition, whether in the form of actions/expectations or structures that imply expectations.

- Families that succeed with continuity planning tend to have a *culture of informed choice*, such that members feel freer to express their choices and voices, but do so with appropriate education and knowledge about finance, law, and other planning-relevant areas.

- *Effective family change agents* exhibit several characteristics including understanding the importance of dreams and relationships in a planning process, emphasis on stewardship, alliance with the family system, and an ability to reframe non-alignment.

- The best leaders of change may not necessarily be founders; rising leaders may be more effective leaders of change.

- If leaders of change are not readily apparent, the family may seek leaders of continuity planning among the extended family or non-family advisors or seek leadership training and mentorship for existing influential members.

CHAPTER 7

Putting It All Together

Recently, I was on my way out of a family wealth conference focused on next-generation leadership when several fellow attendees, rising leaders in their family offices, approached me in the hotel lobby. "I have a question," one of the women said. "At one of the events you mentioned that many continuity plans ultimately fail. What are the most common dysfunctions that lead to those failures?" It was a good question, of course, one that speaks directly to the central message of this book; moreover, it gave me an opportunity to point out something important to the soon-to-be leaders. "Well," I said, "I prefer not think about it in terms of 'dysfunctionality' or 'abnormality.' After all, based on the few statistics we have, the majority of continuity plans don't work out as their developers would hope. So we can think about those families who *succeed* at preserving wealth and family relationships for multiple generations as the abnormal ones! Maybe it would be better for us to be thinking about what underlies the success of those families." That led to a lively discussion about what each of them saw as their families' strengths and successes.

The broader point here is that, as noted throughout this book, *all* families—whether business-owning, wealthy, both, or neither—are confronted by natural forces that work against togetherness and continuity. Fellow family wealth expert Jay Hughes and his colleagues make the point that all families are destined to grow apart eventually, if only due to size alone.[1] Recall

---

[1] James Hughes, Susan Massenzio, and Keith Whitaker, *The Voice of a Rising Generation* (Bloomberg, New York, 2014).

from the *Familyness* chapter our discussion of how much families grow from generation to generation, resulting in dispersal and divergence of places of residence, culture, experience, interests, and values. So it's not whether but *when* family members will move in different directions, straining their ability to create and implement any wealth continuity structures. The good news is that family members today are well-positioned to educate themselves about the process and pitfalls of continuity planning, and to exercise some thoughtful choice in the matter.

In that context, I have made a conscious effort throughout this book not to pathologize differences between families. Just as *within* families some members are more capable of being athletes than others, so *between* families some families are more capable of successfully developing and implementing wealth continuity structures than others might be. Simply because someone wants to be an athlete doesn't mean that he or she can be. And simply because some parties want to implement wealth continuity structures that will preserve wealth and family relationships for generations, does not mean that they can do so effectively. But this is not about abnormality—*it is about differences in capacity.*

The chapters that form the heart of this book delineate the five building blocks that make up a foundation for successful wealth and family preservation, along with practical tips for enhancing these elements in your family or one that you advise. More specifically, I've offered means to:

- enhance *Learning Capacity*
- find a healthy level of *Familyness*
- promote a *Safe Communication Culture*
- enhance *Commitment to Personal Development*
- exercise *Effective Leadership* of Change

At the same time I have discussed the common alternative reality: That a family may not be capable of improvement on a specific building block or set of these, and how best to proceed if that's the case. By refusing to label this reality as "dysfunctional," I hope to make it easier for families to pursue the solutions that work best for them, be it allowing individuals to exit, separating efforts into individual branches, seeking strong consultants or corporate trustees, or other approaches.

I should note that readers may disagree with my proposals for what the building blocks should be in the first place. That's fine. The goal is not to get 100 % agreement on the concept of the Foundation for Family Wealth Continuity and the specific elements it comprises. Rather, I want to get people thinking and talking about the perspective, concepts, and advice contained in this book. Because as I noted in earlier chapters, change occurs when new information is introduced to a system; so whether you agree or disagree, it's about raising the topics here, thinking hard about them, and promoting dialogue that will introduce real, healthy change!

That starts, ideally, with identifying the nature of your family's current Foundation for Family Wealth Continuity.

Assessing Your Family's Foundation for Wealth Continuity

Families are often eager to implement new ideas, whether related to continuity planning, management, governance, or various other matters. But getting the most out of new strategies, approaches, and tactics is impossible unless families and those who advise them understand what they are up against. In the case of building a Foundation for Family Wealth Continuity, that means asking a series of interrelated questions:

- How strong is each building block?
- What can be improved about each?
- How can we improve it?
- What aspects might not be possible to improve?

The answers will help you understand how strong is your overall Foundation, and how each specific building block contributes to the whole. As you might guess, there's no truly accurate measurement tool for each of the building blocks, no barometer or benchmark for these dimensions. That means you have to approach the task of assessment subjectively but in a clear-eyed manner, possibly with the help of outside parties.

Figure 7.1 presents all five building blocks of the Foundation for Family Wealth Continuity and their full range of strength.

In each of the building block chapters are specific criteria to help you understand your family's strength on that particular block. You can use those criteria you develop yourself or with consultants, or some combination to assess the strength of that element, and place an X at the appropriate level on the bars above for each of the blocks. Connecting the X's will provide your family's Foundation profile. An example is illustrated in Fig. 7.2.

Understanding and Addressing Your Family's Foundation for Wealth Continuity

Assessing your family's foundation for wealth continuity is important, but not sufficient to improve your planning and implementation ability. You also have to *understand* what your specific profile means, and how it might be improved. The Fig. 7.2 provides a visual representation of where a sample family stands with regard to each of the building blocks. This family is relatively high with regard to Learning Capacity, Familyness and Safe Communication Culture and relatively low on personal development and effective leadership. As mentioned earlier, these measures are subjective, and may vary based on time and who is doing the measurement. But simply conducting this assessment will provide food for thought and greater potential for open dialogue among family members about important issues. Below I present some of the key patterns and features to look for in your foundation profile.

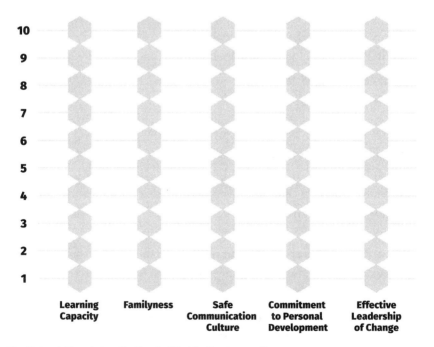

Fig. 7.1   A Foundation for Family Wealth Continuity: Your composite rating

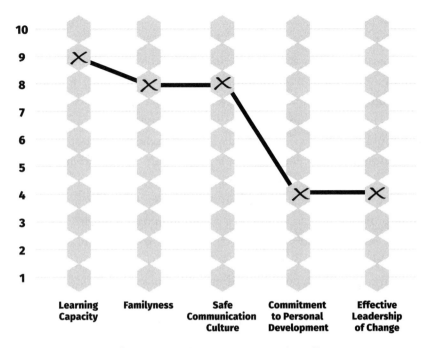

Fig. 7.2 A Foundation for Family Wealth Continuity: Sample Profile

Dips

A particularly low rating on a specific building block—or "dip"—suggests the need to aim family dialogue (perhaps in a family meeting) toward understanding the source of that lower rating and a discussion of the suggestions noted in that specific chapter for improvement. For example, the family with the sample profile above could think about how to promote both personal development and stronger leadership using a combination of educational tactics and external resources.

Multiple dips or troughs

Where several building blocks have low ratings (dips separated by stronger blocks, or "troughs" representing two or more low-rated blocks), it would be best to address the issues in force one at a time. The principle of successive approximations, discussed briefly in the chapter on *Effective Leadership of Change*, is relevant here. That simply means taking small steps in circumscribed areas, rather than trying to change everything at once. Creating a plan to address one low-capacity building block at a time, developing a timeline for addressing the issues, and perhaps even identifying a group or groups of family members to take responsibility for each building block, are possible ways to approach this matter.

Low-capacity profile

An instance of low ratings on all five building blocks, or a low-capacity profile, indicates a family at risk for trying to implement continuity structures or even individual plans with little basis in the reality of the family's overall functioning. For example, a wealth creator who had built a wholesale apparel business in the northeastern US was interested in developing a family office that would serve his long-term needs, along with those of his wife, two adult children from his current marriage, and two adult children from a previous marriage. He had retained an accounting firm to help him put together an elaborate family office structure and system of family governance, but the entire project fell apart within weeks of beginning. When he approached another service provider for help, that provider conducted multiple interviews with family members and pointed out that the family hadn't addressed any of the reasons the project failed in the first place: the children from the two marriages disliked being together; extended family interactions almost always involved pettiness and arguments; the 45-year-old son being groomed to lead the family office had promised to complete an MBA to qualify for the position but hadn't even started the degree; any attempts by the wealth creator to engage the family in continuity planning failed. Still, he insisted on pursuing a conventional plan without resolving any of those issues.

In short, the individual was trying to build an effective continuity structure without a single solid building block. A more realistic approach would have been to promote a dialogue about why creating a family office was so important to him in the first place and whether keeping the family together long-term through that structure was a realistic or even wanted goal.

Spikes

In some cases, a family might be rated very highly on one or two building blocks, or what could be considered "spikes." When such a spike exists, it's important to keep several things in mind. First, it's always a good thing to *recognize and remark upon your family's strengths* or those of one you advise. Business families and families of wealth are often so busy with their enterprise and other activities that members lose sight of the strengths that have made them successful in the first place. One large family I know has developed good structures in their private trust company and works continuously to enhance communication, relationships, and individual skills and talents. Still, they often ask me, "How do other families do this?" Laughing, I usually say, "Other families are looking at *you* to learn how to do this right." So my advice to family leaders is to identify your strengths and take intentional steps to reinforce them and harness them, because they are very important to family members and to the future.

Second, *think about how your strengths can be leveraged to compensate for any weaknesses* in the system. For example, if your leaders have difficulty managing change well (as suggested by a low rating on the effective leadership block), but the family has strong elements of Familyness and Safe Communication Culture, you can feel confident to raise difficult issues of leadership and change without fearing the family will "fall apart" when faced with these. Raising the issues can, in turn, lead to improvement on the lower-capacity building blocks (such as developing stronger leadership).

Finally, it is often a good exercise to *approach a singular strength by asking if something is being lost by emphasis on that one area*. In other words, energy and focus in one area might deplete strength in others. For example, as noted in the chapter on that building block, a spike in Familyness could be accompanied by neglect of individual interests or personal development. One family was so dominated by their focus on Safe Communication Culture every family member was accorded a voice at family meetings—that they neglected the importance of personal development. Regardless of someone's expertise or experience, the family culture emphasized the right to a voice, and many discussions went in circles because there were too many inputs and opinions from those without sufficient understanding or experience with the topic of focus (financial planning, for example).

Building block clusters

You may already have noticed a pattern or clustering among the five building blocks: The first three have more to do with overall family culture ("family culture cluster") and include answers to questions such as "Can we learn and accept feedback?", "Do we like being together?", and "Do we strive toward safe communication?"; the next two ("individual capacity cluster") focus on individual characteristics and strengths: "Do we strive to enhance individual capabilities?" and "Do we benefit from effective leaders?"

It's important to identify cluster-related patterns in your Foundation for Family Wealth Continuity. For example, where the family is uniformly low on the family culture cluster (as illustrated in Fig. 7.3) it may be best to emphasize strengthening individual capacities, since there is a risk in such a family that members will have difficulty supporting each other, and eventually individuals might decide that it would be better for them to pursue their own interests, rather than focus on collective continuity.

To illustrate, a 70-year-old manufacturing family business in the Pacific Northwest had striven to ensure continuity over the years by limiting the contribution of in-laws (they couldn't work in the business or own shares) and by regulating ownership options strictly (beyond the restriction on in-laws, only those actually working in the business could be shareholders). These requirements helped keep the family in the business but undermined Learning Capacity (the seniors refused to consider broader ownership options), interfered with Familyness (in-laws were considered outsiders), and contributed to unsafe communication (ownership issues were considered off the table in family meetings). This family was bound together mostly by structure, not by family culture. Although there certainly should be effort applied to enhancing the building blocks in the family culture cluster, it would be important in a family such as this to ensure that individuals are competent and capable of standing on their own (Commitment to Personal Development), due to lack of family support. There should also be an emphasis on developing effective leadership, as the leaders in this family are faced with the task of aligning family members in a context that provides little choice and not much engagement among members.

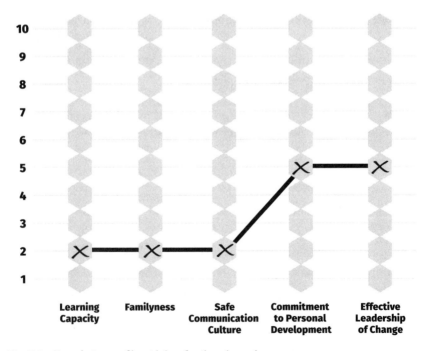

Fig. 7.3   Foundation profile with low family-culture cluster

On the other hand, a family with a strong family culture cluster might enjoy on-going harmony and positive relationships, along with a collective interest in continuity. But relative weakness on the individual capacity cluster might prevent the group from nurturing strong knowledge or leadership at the individual level, making it difficult to implement continuity plans effectively. So it's about understanding such trade-offs between family and individual and taking steps to shore up areas of deficit while also being realistic about what's possible in the future.

The Journey Ahead

As part of my final thoughts for you, I should emphasize again that the most important part of assessing the strength of your Foundation for Family Wealth Continuity is not to identify the exact "truth" about your family status—which is typically a moving target anyway—but to spark conversation, to engage family members around critical matters, and to stimulate action in key areas related to the family's future.

In that context, I hope that you as readers have benefited from the content here in several ways:

1. *Understanding that wealth continuity structures do not stand alone.* Wealth continuity structures *always* exist in a context of family dynamics. If the family is poorly engaged, unprepared, or unsupportive, then the structure, no matter how "technically" correct, is unlikely to accomplish the goal of keeping family and assets together.

2. *Avoiding fascination with continuity structures.* A logical extension of the point above is that it's important not to over-emphasize structures, especially fancy ones with lots of bells and whistles. They may be enticing and even appropriate in the right family situation, but the family context must be considered carefully before any attempt to implement even the simplest structure.

3. *Recognizing that the Foundation and its building blocks represent just one approach.* The model presented here of a foundation comprising five building blocks is just one way of approaching and understanding the family context for wealth continuity planning or any other important effort (such as building governance structures). There are certainly other approaches, and the concepts here are best used in conjunction with those and, often with inputs from outside experts.

4. *Knowing when change is not possible.* We have discussed many suggestions for how to enhance the building blocks, but also how to proceed if such improvement seems impossible, whether for a single block or the entire Foundation. I have seen many cases of families "throwing good effort after bad" when there was little possibility of change in the first place. So it's important to be realistic about what can happen in your family, and make the best of your situation regardless.

Wherever your family or one you advise may be with regard to the strength of a Foundation for Family Wealth Continuity, it's critical to understand that the journey to effective planning and long-term continuity will almost definitely have many bumps, road-blocks, and unexpected detours along the way. As with many aspects of family business, it's more about a willingness to take the trip and face those challenges with head and heart, than about a focus on the final destination. Indeed, for families with the strongest interest in and foundation for continuity planning, there may be no true future end-point, just the inspiration to keep building and growing wealth, family engagement, and harmony, for many generations to come.

Points to Remember

Here are the key points from this chapter that puts everything else in the book together:

- Wealth continuity planning is difficult for the vast majority of families, because natural forces lead to dispersal of members' interests and goals. Some families are naturally better than others at planning, and those that struggle should not be pathologized but encouraged to build a stronger foundation for planning and to recognize the limits of potential improvement.
- The first step to improving a Foundation for Family Wealth Continuity is *assessment* of the Foundation's current strength, based on the unique profile of strengths and weaknesses among the building blocks.
- *Understanding and addressing* the Foundation for Family Wealth Continuity involves recognizing specific patterns and features:
  - *Dips and troughs*, or low-rated blocks or sets of blocks, can be addressed using ideas from chapters devoted to those specific blocks.

- A *low-capacity profile*, or a Foundation with minimal strength, suggests the family may struggle to maintain continuity and needs to understand that such a goal may not be feasible or wanted.
- *Spikes*, or strengths on individual blocks, should be recognized, reinforced, and harnessed to promote continuity and other positive family features, while not being over-emphasized at the expense of other blocks.
- *Building block clusters* may represent strength related to family culture or individual capacities. Families should understand each cluster represents a trade-off between family and individual interests/capabilities, and work to address deficits while maintaining a realistic view on what's possible.
- The journey to continuity, though rewarding, is not easy, and success is more about a desire and willingness to improve the Foundation through careful attention to the building blocks, frank conversations about the need for improvement, and an ongoing commitment to healthy dialogue and meaningful action.

Index

A
alignment, 118
altruism, 57–8
apathy, 126–7
Aronoff, Craig, 35n13, 138n7

B
be my clone syndrome, 28
best practices, 5, 72
Bowen, Murray, 52, 52n7

C
closed system, 25, 69
Collier, Charles, 101, 101n3
Columbo approach, 135
Commitment to Personal
    Development, 13, 93–116, 95f
conflict, 49–50, 78, 82

D
delay of gratification, 104
destructive entitlement, 50
diversity, 29, 51
dreams, 133
Duncan, John, 42, 42n1
dysfunction, 143

E
Effective Leadership of Change,
    14, 117–42, 140f
emotional intelligence, 103–8
empathy, 81–2, 92, 104, 105
entropy, 50n5
Erikson, Erik, 73, 73n2
exceptions, 135–6

F
family dynamics, 123
Familyness, 13, 41–64
feedback, 31–2, 83–6, 92
financial literacy, 101–2
financial skills, 101
four horsemen, 79–81, 92

G
generosity, 111–12
Godfrey, Jolene, 101, 101n4
Goleman, Daniel, 107, 107n10
Gottman, John, 79, 79n5
gratitude, 111

H
health and happiness, 116

Note: Figures are referred to by italicized "f"

homeostasis, 123, 124
Hughes, James E., 50, 50n5

I
implementation, 7, 121, 135
imposed mutuality, 48
inclusiveness, 58–9
inertia, 126–7
informed choice, 130–3
intention/outcome discrepancy, 85
intimacy, 55

J
Jung, Carl, 76, 76n4

L
Learning Capacity, 13, 17–40
learning organization, 19, 19n2, 20
levels of intimacy, 60–1, 61*f*
listening, 36–7

M
magic ratio, the, 79–80
Maister, David, 75
mastery/self efficacy, 112
mindfulness, 112

N
narcissism, 24–7

P
primogeniture, 42
psychological reactance, 127–9

R
reconciliation, 68
reframe, 136

S
Safe Communication Culture,
   13, 65–92, 68*f,* 89*f*
self regulation, 104
Senge, Peter, 19, 19n1
social skill, 104
stewardship, 133
successive approximations, 125
systems, 121–3

T
triangulation, 78
trust, 11, 17–19, 73–6, 92

U
underlying factors, 124, 142

V
vision, 9, 134
voice, 87, 92, 131

W
Ward, John, 133n5
wealth continuity planning,
   2–3, 152
wealth continuity structure,
   8–10, 151
Why questions, 71–3

Printed in the United States of America